Saving the Best for Last:
Creating Our Lives After 50

Renée Fisher

Saving the Best for Last: Creating Our Lives After 50

Renee Fisher
Joyce Kramer
Jean Peelen

Authors of *Invisible No More: The Secret Lives of Women Over 50*

iUniverse, Inc.
New York Bloomington

Saving the Best for Last: Creating Our Lives After 50

iUniverse books may be ordered through booksellers or by contacting:

iUniverse
1663 Liberty Drive
Bloomington, IN 47403
www.iuniverse.com
1-800-Authors (1-800-288-4677)

Because of the dynamic nature of the Internet, any Web addresses or links contained in this book may have changed since publication and may no longer be valid. The views expressed in this work are solely those of the author and do not necessarily reflect the views of the publisher, and the publisher hereby disclaims any responsibility for them.

ISBN: 978-1-4401-3374-9 (pbk)
ISBN: 978-1-4401-3375-6 (ebk)

Printed in the United States of America

iUniverse rev. date: 4/13/2009

This book is dedicated to all women, wherever they may be on their journey, and to all the women and men who supported us on our journey.

CONTENTS

Dear Reader

Like many of you, we are women who are in the second part of our lives. Our journeys have taken us through the best life has to offer and occasionally what seemed like the worst. When we passed the threshold of fifty, we moved from commiserating about wrinkles to being energized about the prospect of having whole new lives ahead of us. We came to believe that we are the generation that is redesigning the meaning of life after fifty.

In our previous book, ***Invisible No More: The Secret Lives of Women Over 50***, we wrote about our experiences and hoped that other women who read about our experiences could see their lives reflected in ours. Our goal was to present fifty as something new: fifty is not merely a milestone to cross. Fifty is not the beginning of the end.

The response from readers was overwhelming. Women not only saw themselves in the pages of our book, but they were inspired to take their lives on in ways that we could never have anticipated. Women got the courage they needed to end damaging relationships and move forward. Others discovered they were worthy enough to commit to new, healthy relationships. Many women got the courage to finally deal with sexual abuse that had occurred decades ago and discovered that they had survived. Women quit jobs, got new ones, took round-the-world trips, displayed their paintings, cut their hair, went back to school, or healed family relationships. Many simply called family members and friends and expressed their love and gratitude. Most importantly, thousands of women actually started to look forward to the years to come.

As thrilled as we were by the constant feedback, we came to believe that there existed the possibility of something even more powerful. So we decided to write a follow up book, one that would incorporate the stories we told in the first but would take our message to a higher level. In this new book, our stories are no longer the focus. They are simply the jumping off point for what follows. We began by adding several new chapters, chapters that should have been included in the first book.

The heart of *Saving the Best for Last: Creating Our Lives After 50* is the individual and group activities that follow each chapter. We never thought of these as discussion questions or workbook-type exercises. Instead, they are powerful, mini-workshops that allow women, whether alone or in group settings, to see their lives in a completely new way, from a completely new perspective. We promise you, the reader, that you will never have experienced anything like this before.

We have created resources and a bibliography section that you can find on our Web page: www.invisiblenomore.com. It is designed to be with you long after the book is completed and will continue to add to your life for many years to come.

We three continue on this journey, one that never ceases to perplex us or frustrate us at times. But at no time is it any less than remarkable, and at no time do we ever wish we were on any journey other than our own. We invite you to join us.

How to Read This Book

The joy of *Saving the Best for Last* is that you can approach your experience of it in any way you choose. Whatever chapter you open to is where you may start your journey. The way you choose to read and use this book is up to you.

A wonderful choice you have is to record your own life story though the assignment at the end of each chapter. This is your opportunity to explore your past, present, and future in depth, and to leave a legacy for your friends and family.

And finally, you have a choice as to whether to take this journey alone or invite your friends to go on the journey with you. While self-exploration is an activity that doesn't require a group, be aware that sharing this experience with other women can greatly enrich your own experience. You may wish to invite your friends, or study group, or church group, or book club to join you.

However you decide to move ahead, please read carefully the instructions for all exercises. These exercises are intended to assist you to uncover possibilities in your own life. As such, they may lead to "Aha!" moments, and sometimes may trigger pain you would rather not recall. Both are valuable experiences. So allow yourself sufficient time to complete the exercises and, if possible, create a space in which you can work uninterrupted through a topic.

Most important, know that you are not alone. Your journey is one shared by the countless women over fifty who are rediscovering their dreams, creating the futures they want, and living as the authors of their lives. Welcome to the club.

Comments About Age

Why start this book with comments about age? Because aging is the reality of our lives. It is the natural process that, more than anything else, impacts our thoughts and actions. We have the ability to control virtually every other aspect of our lives but this.

The aging process is twofold. It is the inexorable deterioration of cellular structure, muscle tone, and our bodies' natural ability to recover from injury. We may notice that bruises take more time to heal; brown spots begin to appear on our hands, wrinkles occur around our mouths and eyes. We may wince as we stand up after being seated for awhile or our backs may ache after driving many miles. We may get a bit winded after hiking well-loved trails or dancing to well-loved music.

Gradually, we give up mini-skirts, and tight sweaters, and high heels. We get used to sensible shoes and bras with good support. We may hear "Oh, you haven't aged at all," but we know that the speaker hasn't seen us when we got out of bed that morning.

As we become more sensitive to the onslaught of age on our bodies, many of the people we deal with in our lives suddenly begin to look like our own children. Many of us who are still out in the workforce realize that we no longer look like everyone else around us. We watch younger and younger people being hired, and we attend more and more retirement parties for people who, from our vantage point, look too young to retire.

The media present us with a model of appearance that we left behind decades ago. Even magazines geared to "women over forty" show an array of women who may be forty but who are little over. Fifty is as far away from these women as thirty.

The other side of the aging coin is one that cannot be measured by physicians' eye charts or bone joint MRIs. It is a gradual awakening for many of us that as we get older, we gain an insight into life that youth did not allow. Age, unlike popular belief, does not bestow automatic wisdom. But it does give perspective. We can dislike what age does to our bodies while at the same time, we can like *ourselves* much more. Many of us have discovered the headiness of coming to terms with the outward manifestations of aging. Others of us have declared if not a truce with the aging process, then at least a temporary standoff. We will continue to grow, to evolve, and to love our lives while at the same time staring at the mirror each morning, having to reacquaint ourselves with ourselves.

We three, like all women, alternately laugh about, cry over, or try to ignore the passage of time. We have loved our faces and bodies; we have been frustrated by our faces and bodies. We have come to an accommodation that might result in cosmetic surgery or merely in softer lighting. Through it all, we have realized that the mirror has no power in itself. The mirror, like any other experience in life, merely reflects what we expect it to. The gift, at this stage of our lives, is that we get to change the expectations.

RENEE

My Aunt Gert reminds me at regular intervals that last year a stranger at the supermarket struck up a flirtatious conversation with her in the checkout line. When the subject of age came up, my aunt announced that she was eighty years old. The man, apparently shocked by this admission, replied that he thought she was no older than sixty-five. "I'll kiss, but I won't do anything else," my Aunt Gert added. The stranger completed his purchase, disappeared into the crowd, and was never seen again. No doubt to find more fertile hunting grounds.

My aunt often bemoans the fact that men "all want the same thing," and she doesn't understand why she can't find one who would be satisfied solely with occasional kisses and the pleasure of chauffeuring her around. But underneath her complaints, I believe she feels indebted to the supermarket stranger. He bestowed upon her the evidence she needed to give herself a fifteen-year age discount. And my aunt, like virtually every other mature woman, wants to look younger than her age.

"You don't look your age."

From age five to just under age thirty, this comment borders on insult. From ages thirty to fifty, the same comment morphs into a compliment. Past age fifty, for many women it can be a veritable lifeboat, sent to save them from the shark-infested waters of decrepitude.

Up to age twenty-something, growing older is synonymous with the acquisition of independence and sexual appeal. Each year brings new delights: bigger, stronger, taller, and curvier. Hips sway, voices drop, breasts pop, as do the eyes of the men on the street who pass us by. We discover a type of power we never experienced before and the result is intoxicating.

Past age thirty, accumulating that "mature" look is, for the most part, no longer necessary for any of the above. Unless we are running for political office, looking older isn't much of an asset. And, as far as sex appeal goes, the popular media doesn't give extra points for the years accumulated beyond that magic moment when "girl" becomes "woman."

As I approached fifty, the comment: "You don't look your age," became an oasis to the desert wanderer. "You don't look your age," was a validation that, unlike every other poor slob on the planet, I was impervious to the aging process. I began to notice more and more of my peers declaring that they didn't look their age, that they were proud of how "young" they looked, and how everyone else thought they looked "so much younger" than they really were. I, too, beamed when people told me I didn't look my age. Sure, I may have occasionally forgotten what I was supposed to be doing at any moment of the day, but I remembered every single person who told me that I didn't look my age. I collected such remarks like fine silver. I polished them and placed them on display.

Then, gradually, I began to have a disconnect. How can I be proud of who I am if I spend so much energy asserting that I look otherwise? How can I call myself a powerful woman when I don't own who and what I am?

My realization crystallized with the death of my close friend, Miki, the year each of us turned forty-seven. When Miki died, my notion of age shifted from one of burden to one of joy. Each year, each moment, became a gift. Each of my birthdays was a birthday that Miki would never have. I decided to commemorate all of my future birthdays for both of us.

Then and there my goal would be to own my age, whatever that age might be. I would embrace aging, rather than flee it. It was up to me to create whatever meaning my age had. It would be my way to honor Miki.

When people used to tell me that I didn't look my age, my answer was, "Thank you." Those people were obviously paying me a compliment. Now, when I hear such compliments, I smile and say, "This is what sixty looks like." It has become very important to me to be a great example of the age I am, rather than an imitation of another age.

If I stop trying to look like someone else's age, I can make my age, whatever it is, fabulous. I can set new standards for whatever age I am. I can keep raising the bar as I raise the numbers. I can change the world as well as my hair color.

I choose to declare to the world the power and knock-your-socks-off sex appeal of whatever age I am. I am sixty. I truly believe that sixty doesn't look like anything, except who and what I am and the unlimited potential that I have. Right now. At this moment. That is the true definition of being ageless. I create the meaning of my age.

JOYCE

Aging has never been about diminishing physical appearance or whether I look my age. Aging, for me, is not about numbers. While I do care about my looks and fret sometimes over the wrinkles, aging means much more to me. Aging is growing wiser, putting my past behind me, and being fully alive. Aging means healing and maturing on the inside, accepting myself and who I am.

I grew up with low self-esteem. At age five, I got down on my knees in the middle of the night when I couldn't sleep and prayed to God to make me look like Elizabeth Taylor. I prayed my freckles would go away; prayed my plain, straight, stringy brown hair would be replaced with rich, shiny, curly black hair; and prayed my boring brown eyes would be replaced with jewel blue eyes to match Elizabeth's. She was my idol, the ultimate in female beauty. I, on the other hand, I was a homely and ugly duckling.

I used that very adjective "homely" to describe myself into adulthood. I picked up this notion, I'm sure, from my father who called me all sorts of unflattering names such as "bag of bones," "freckles," "skinny," "ugly," and others since forgotten. The most important man in my life said these things about me. His words were indelibly etched in my mind.

I held onto my strong belief that I was unattractive. Yet, when I review events and facts of my life, the evidence proves I was wrong about how I viewed myself. But facts did not have the power to counter beliefs that began in early childhood. Facts could not, and did not, alter my self-image.

When I married in my early twenties, my husband expressed his appreciation of my face and body. No matter what he said, though, I still didn't believe that I was attractive. I heard the words but never felt the emotion.

In my forties, I began to get a glimmer of my own personal power and magnetism. Through counseling, I was able to begin claiming all that was rightfully mine: attractiveness, sexiness, desirability, freedom of expression, and a growing awareness of my extraordinary ability to connect with people. I recognized the depth of my compassion for others and my ability to make a difference in the world by being who I was. I noticed then that when I looked in the mirror, I saw a person I had never seen before, and it was me! I was beginning to see a woman whose face I liked—and it was mine!

During my forties when I was politically active in the teachers' union, organizing a collective bargaining unit, and running a citywide campaign for an elected school board, I noticed that people, both men and women, were drawn to me. I dated a number of them. I just couldn't get over how I was "suddenly" attractive to others.

As I turned fifty, I experienced myself as the most beautiful woman I had ever been in my life because at fifty I liked myself. Liking me coincided with my discovery of the ingredients that make me attractive to others.

I have learned my appeal and charm come from my own sense

of self: my delight in, and love of, who I am; my sense of purpose in life; my joy and passion; my willingness to take risks; my stand for my principles; and my gratitude for all the blessings of my life, especially that I'm alive.

This is not to say that I don't appreciate compliments about my appearance. Recently my ex-husband said to me, "You're certainly aging gracefully." I chose to hear in his comment several things: "You look good," "You're attractive," and "You've softened."

I attract others when I am attractive to myself, when I love myself. I love my face. I love the smile and laugh lines around my eyes and mouth, the creases around my cheeks where my face crinkles into a smile. I cannot begin to count the hundreds of times people I don't know have paused when passing me on the street or in the hall or elevator to tell me how beautiful my smile is. I love to hear that. My face tells it all.

JEAN

I was never a beauty. I was tall and skinny. All I had to do was look around my junior high school class to see the differences between my classmates and me. They had shiny beautiful hair, soft-looking shapely bodies, and clear skin. I was five feet nine inches in the seventh grade. I had acne, a home perm, a flat chest, and a jutting jaw line. I had a desire to be one of the pretty girls, but I also had a desire to be rich, and I was very clear that I wasn't rich.

Given that I wasn't going to get through life on a beauty pass, I didn't then have to waste time playing with things like make-up, fashion, and hairstyles. I could play girl's basketball and run for class president. A ponytail worked all the way to college. I had lots of girlfriends and no boyfriends. This left a lot of time to develop my own way of becoming who I wanted to be in the world. Since I also didn't think I was very smart, I decided I had better be the kind of person who people wanted around. My ticket to what I wanted was energy, life, and laughter.

Turning fifty, for me, did not involve the fear of the loss of beauty. I did, however, fear losing youth. I noted when I turned fifty that I, who had depended on my very high energy, was being greeted too frequently with, "Hey, are you tired?" The mirror showed me that the top parts of my upper eyelids were sagging over the lower parts. I did look tired, or sick, or bored, or something. I did not look energetic, alive, and on the move.

At that time, I was an executive in a government agency whose work was controversial and in the public eye. I was negotiating with state and local education agencies, and I was speaking at major legal conferences around the country. I was concerned that professionally I would be seen as done, washed up, tired, on the way to retirement.

So, I started reading about cosmetic surgery. Cosmetic surgery then was not as accepted or common as it is now. I probably knew a number of women who had had eye jobs, or nose jobs, but they didn't talk about it. They just "went on vacation" for a couple of weeks and reappeared looking refreshed and renewed.

I suspected, even then, that cosmetic surgery would soon not be such a big deal: that we would think of having our eyes done in the same way we thought about having braces on our teeth. Yes, cosmetic surgery was inherently more dangerous because it was surgery, but an eye job did not require general anesthesia, only some great drugs that made me not care what the surgeon was doing.

I had my eyelids fixed. I only stayed out of work for about one week and then returned looking dramatic in my rhinestone shades. I was bruised around the eyes, but otherwise fairly normal. I decided not to make a secret of the surgery and found that just about everyone was fascinated with the subject, male and female alike.

I loved my eye job. Comments came unsolicited: "You look great!" or "Been on vacation?" Now my outside matched my inside: wide awake, high energy, interested, and interesting. I didn't have to worry any more about a silly thing like eye-lid droop interfering with my career trajectory.

In my mid-fifties, people began to tell me I was pretty. What an odd thing! I couldn't understand what was happening. I never had been pretty, and this was supposed to be the era of disintegration. My body was doing some age-related things like varicose veins, and softening of the chin line; yet, people seemed to be giving me the message that, for the first time in my life, I was pretty. Beyond removing the tired eyes, nothing physical had changed, yet peoples' perception of me had changed. I looked in the mirror.

What I saw, and what I knew, was that for the first time in my life I was at peace with myself. My forties had been hard. I had been a tough, self-sufficient, ambitious woman. My early fifties brought a desire to have more and less: more depth to my life and less isolation. My view of life shifted. I had always been a tough, strong, accomplished woman. Now I was becoming a vulnerable, loving woman.

It was my transformation that was showing in my face. Worry lines were gone, defensiveness was gone, and hardness was gone. The barriers were down. Because I was no longer responsible for making sure that my opinion prevailed, or that everything got done "right," I was calmer. I had more time to think about, and pay attention to, others. That is what people saw and liked. They called it pretty, but my look was actually inviting.

So now when people comment about my age, "Gee, you don't look your age," or "You look good for your age," I just say, "Thank you." What I now know is that there is no beauty secret. If you want cosmetic surgery, special creams or lotions, they are all available. But true beauty comes from a peaceful spirit within.

YOUR TURN
Discussion Questions:
1. At what age did you suddenly feel "not young?" Describe your experience. Is it important to you to be seen as younger than you are? Why?
2. Does your view of yourself today differ from that of when you were younger? If so, how has your view changed? Why? What do you miss most about the younger you?
3. What do you look forward to with respect to aging? What do you dread the most?

Individual Exercise: *See Beauty*
1. Make a list of three famous women you think are beautiful inside and out. After each name, write three things you think make her beautiful.
2. Now name three things about yourself that make you beautiful. Do NOT question the premise that you are beautiful.
3. Compare the two lists. Are the items on each list similar or different? Do you possess qualities you admire in others? Does the "ideal" you see in others seem within your reach, or is it unobtainable? Does your list of ideal women represent what you are, or what you are *not*? Are you kinder to them than you are to yourself? Why?
4. In large letters on a sheet of clean paper, write the three qualities that make you beautiful. Tape this poster to your mirror. Leave it there for thirty days. When you look at yourself in the morning, or if self-doubt creeps in, read your list. Acknowledge your own beauty.

Group Exercise: *How Others See Us*
This exercise needs a group leader.
The purpose of this exercise is to get feedback as to how much we care about how others judge our age.
1. Each person makes a list with the name of every person in the group, including herself. Do not, in any way, identify who is writing the list.
2. After each person's name, write your best guess of her age. If you already know a person's age, just put it down without

comment. Be truthful, do not attempt to flatter.

3. Compile the ages by person, so that each person has feedback on how others see her. Put each person, and a list of all the ages guessed for her, on new pieces of paper—one person per sheet of paper. Hand the papers out to the individuals.

4. Then discuss the following:

    *   Before you saw the feedback, how anxious were you about how old others think you are? Why does it matter?

    *   Were people accurate in their guesses about you? Were you surprised in any way?

    *   How did you feel when you looked at your results? Does this feedback make any difference in your life? In what way?

Assignment:

Pretend you are the fourth author of *Saving the Best for Last* and write your "Comments About Age" in your notebook.

Accepting Our Bodies

If we are like most women, we reach a point where we must acknowledge what many of us think of as our bodies turning on us. If we have taken care of them, eaten the right food, exercised, stayed out of the sun, the deterioration may be minimal. But it is there nonetheless. If we live, we deteriorate. If we have been cavalier in the care of our bodies, we may be shocked to discover that fat seems to cling more tenaciously, our energy levels go down faster than our age would indicate, and our skin looks far older than our age. We regret every slice of pepperoni pizza, every year we deferred gym membership, every summer we thought a tan would be a great thing to have.

But there it is. We are at midlife or beyond, and sometimes it seems that our bodies are galloping way ahead of us into old age. We say, "But I feel young!" while new aches and pains attack our bodies. We feel more and more like some alien being has taken over that has nothing to do with us, the *real* us.

At some point, we get to stop. We get to acknowledge that our bodies, for better or worse, are here for the long haul. Unless medical science comes up with a way to trade them in, we had better start to arrange for some kind of truce. We can think of ourselves as prisoners in aging bodies, or we can take ownership of them. The most fortunate of us have crossed over into pure love of every wrinkle, every sag, every discomfort, every pound. Our bodies, for better or worse, remind us every day that we are alive and how we view them is a pretty good indication of how we view our lives.

RENEE

I have little memory of health. From age three on, the doctor always seemed to be coming to my house to treat me for measles, chicken pox, mumps, colds, flu. I battled pneumonia and a constant stream of ear, nose, and throat infections. I missed almost all of second grade. I remember spending days in my parents' bed, listening to the radio. Each illness validated my increasing belief that there was something terribly deficient about me. And there didn't seem to be anything I could do about it.

By age ten, the comments about my posture started. "Stand up straight," everyone would say. I didn't understand why I had to struggle to do that. Wasn't standing up straight something that should come naturally, like the ability to blink one's eyes or roll one's head from side to side? And wasn't a beautifully arched spine part of being a dancer? Being a ballet dancer had been my dream since age three, and I continued to take ballet lessons, believing I would outgrow my difficulty.

In my early twenties, an x-ray of my spine, taken for another reason entirely, revealed spina bifida, a gap in the spinal column, as well as a forward curvature. Nonetheless, twenty years after my last childhood ballet lesson, I tried to take an adult ballet class. I still remember the moment when I realized I could no longer bend over or balance properly. I then consulted an orthopedic surgeon. This one had a diagnosis: Scheuermann's Disease, a congenital deformity of the spine that manifests itself in puberty and results in a progressive forward curvature. The doctor advised against surgery because of the danger involved in working so close to the spinal chord. While I contemplated surgery anyway, my allergies continued to worsen. I spent my time focused on chronic bronchitis, asthmatic bronchitis, and numerous sinus infections. Again, I saw each illness as a test of my "normalcy," a test I invariably failed.

During my forties, continuing pains and disabling symptoms sent me from specialist to specialist. I gathered diagnoses and medical bills. Finally, an orthopedic surgeon told me that all of my symptoms were due to the increasing curvature of my spine.

This time around, I opted for a surgical procedure that would place two titanium rods down the length of my spine. I was fifty years old, and I didn't care how difficult the surgery would be or how much pain would be involved. All I wanted was to be normal. My whole life, it seemed, was a failure to be like other people, physically. I was beginning to deal positively with the issues in my personal life, and I was now ready to take on the largest issue in my physical being. The surgery was difficult, but I believe I made the right decision.

Two years after the surgery, I went with a group of friends to Maui. The flight was long and sitting in the airplane seat was extremely painful. I felt myself lapsing once again into self-pity over my physical condition.

In Maui, Jean and I attended an art show and strolled under a legendary banyan tree in the heart of town. We stopped by the display of a man who created exquisite Japanese-inspired watercolors with pen and ink messages inscribed. The messages were beautiful, haunting, and most of all intriguing.

My eye caught an exceptionally small, delicate painting of an orchid, pale pink against textured rag paper. I had to look closely to see what was written underneath. The message, in tiny inked script, read: "I am not this fragile body." I stood in front of it, and I cried. Fifty-two years and thousands of miles had brought me to this one moment in time, this one message, shaded under the spreading arms of the banyan.

I cried for the athlete I would never be. I cried for the dancer I would never be. I cried for races never run and bikes never ridden and trails never hiked. I cried for the school races I had lost and for the schoolyard teams nobody chose me for. Most of all, I cried because the message I was reading was so difficult for me to internalize. I had always defined myself by my failure to stand tall, to run, to jump, to balance myself on a bike, to throw a ball. I cried and I cried because I could do nothing but cry.

When we returned from Maui, Jean presented me with a gift. Inside the box was the small painting, the "I am not this fragile body" painting. I cried all over again, and I put the painting up on the wall next to my desk at home. I have lost track of how many times I have looked at it in the years since.

In those rare moments that I allow the painting to speak to me, I know that I really am something more than the sum total of my physical condition. I am the small girl whose pre-adolescent body could soar in ballet class, grown now to the woman whose mind soars daily to heights never imagined possible by the small girl.

In those moments, I no longer mourn for that young ballet dancer. Instead, I am filled with gratitude for what life has given me and for what I am capable of giving to life. I do not see the aging process as a betrayal of my body. My body has not betrayed me because I never was my body. I have been and always will be something more. My youthful vitality had nothing to do with flexibility and muscles, any more than it did with my firm breasts and unlined face. My vitality now is not diminished by the absence of any of those. I am the woman I have always been and will continue to be. And more if I wish. Much more. I am not this fragile body.

JOYCE

Growing up, I never liked anything about my body and how I looked. When a younger sister started her period before I did, it proved something was wrong with me internally as well.

Experiencing sexual abuse by my father created a dislike for my body and how it could be misused. It wasn't that I didn't want to be a girl. It was that I was not like other girls. My body was a trap. It held my pain, resentment, fear, worthlessness, and rage, and I could not escape it. Since I did not like my body, it followed that I did not like myself. I thought I was not normal.

When I turned eighteen and left home, I was free of my father, but I was still in my body. When it refused to experience orgasms, I thought it was my body's fault, another malfunction. As I moved into my forties, I experienced my body betraying me in other ways. I required a hysterectomy, my breasts sagged, and my hot flashes went on and on. If I hadn't liked my body when I was younger, how was I supposed to like it now that it was coming apart at the seams? In my secret thoughts, I felt my body was a cruel joke.

This outlook about my physical appearance and internal dysfunction was self- centered. I cared only about looking good and putting up a front to the world. I didn't sleep enough, eat properly, exercise, and I smoked. I rarely engaged in stress reducing activities. So, while I did not accept myself, I also did nothing to change my harmful habits.

When I was diagnosed with breast cancer, I was confronted with my mortality, my unhealthiness, and my attitude that my life did not matter. I was not convinced it mattered if I was on the planet. As I moved through an intense period of self-examination, I saw my lifelong, consistent refusal to acknowledge my personal being as important. Most of my life I devalued my body, yet it had served as my armor: I hated being in it, but I used it to steel me emotionally for survival.

I also began to appreciate the powerful relationship of physical, mental, and spiritual health. Intense scrutiny enabled me to uncover my personal beliefs and their influence on my attitudes and lifestyle. The beliefs that enabled me to survive my childhood no longer served me as an adult. To change my life, I had to change my beliefs. At this juncture, I chose to believe that I did matter and that taking care of me was a number one priority. Embracing these beliefs changed my perspective on life and spurred me into action.

What began to matter now was being healthy. I discovered that I wanted to live, not simply to exist. I wanted to thrive, not simply to survive. I quit smoking. I started getting more sleep and focused my attention on nutrition. I learned how to relax. I went to dances. I made time for my family and friends. I left my unsatisfying job and moved to another city. I took responsibility for creating a healthy lifestyle.

I shifted my obsession with my outward appearance to addressing my health. I set a goal to create a balanced life—or as close to one as I could get. These days I have a sense of well being as I address my needs and holistically nurture and care about myself.

I was well into my fifties before I fully appreciated my body, mind, and spirit and all they are capable of doing. One part is no longer separate from the other. The sum of me is greater than my parts.

JEAN

When I was close to fifty, I decided to get a tattoo—a tiny little rose. It would be a symbol of my frequent desire to flout the norms. It would be thumbing my nose at fifty.

I had never given much thought to my body. In youth, I took its healthy state for granted. It just worked like it was supposed to. But I was a heavy smoker for thirty years. I had developed a smoker's cough and wheezy lungs. I was a red wine and Johnny Walker Red scotch drinker who eased my way from work to bed every night with too many drinks. I almost never missed work because of alcohol; and my career path was still going upward, but I often went to work with the haze of the night before still swishing around my brain. When I went out for the evening and drank, I repeatedly put myself (and others) in danger by driving drunk.

What was going on? The interesting thing was that I really didn't *know*. I could see that I was engaging in behaviors destined to shorten my life. I was, however, in full-fledged denial that I could be an alcoholic. My daughters once tried their own mini-intervention with me, telling me they were worried about me and thought I had a problem with alcohol. I dismissed them through a two-step process: denial and attack. I told them I couldn't be an alcoholic because I did not have an alcoholic personality. I was not whiney and needy. I was confident and strong and achieving and happy. I then told them they had enough of their own problems they might want to concentrate on. Coming from Mom, that can be a zinger.

So, I ignored them. And I got a rose tattoo. It seemed easier than really trying to understand what was going on in my life.

When I went for the tattoo, I had several scotches to ease the fear and pain that (believe you me) is a big part of getting a tattoo. Trouble arose, however, as the tattoo artist was also drinking one scotch for every one I drank. He got drunk and, as a result, couldn't color within the lines. When the great unveiling of the tiny rose came, what was revealed was a blurry blob with leaves. I ranted at him to no avail as there was nothing to be done. The laser removal process was, at least at that time, prohibitively expensive and would result in some ugly scars. The only alternative was to let this tattoo fully heal, and then go to another tattoo artist to create a design that would cover the blob. That is how I ended up with two roses, vines, leaves, and a butterfly—all on my right breast.

In June of 1993, sick of coughing and hacking, and beginning to worry about permanent body damage from smoking, I decided to try to quit. I was sent to the Federal Executive Institute, in Charlottesville, Virginia, for a month-long executive training program. At the Institute, they offered a smoking cessation program as well as an alcohol-counseling program. I decided to take on one thing, the smoking, just to see if I could do it. I was half-hearted about the commitment. My "buddy" in the program was also shaky about his own commitment. We compared notes and shared the commiserations and justifications of the about-to-fails.

That same evening I was attending a softball game and my buddy was sitting up behind me, at the top of the bleachers. Suddenly there was a thump, and then exclamations of distress. I looked back to see that my buddy had fallen backward off the bleachers. We rushed over to him and someone started CPR. A heart attack had caused him to fall.

My stop-smoking buddy lived. He survived the heart attack. And I never smoked another cigarette. It was hard to quit. It was hell to quit. And it took someone almost dying in front of my eyes to have me know I wanted to live, but I got it. I would go through anything to live. Within two months, my lungs started clearing. I could take deep breaths without wheezing or coughing. My smoker's hack disappeared. I began to take pride in the health and resilience of my body.

By taking on that one fear and making it through, and by experiencing the physical rewards for quitting smoking, the next challenge became less scary, less difficult. Within months of quitting smoking, I finally ended my thirteen-year dysfunctional relationship. It wasn't neat or clean. It was ugly and hurtful and it dragged out; but, it was clear to me that it was over, and I had the strength to make it so. The man I lived with said to me, much after the break-up when it had become less painful to talk to each other, "I knew when you quit smoking that my days were numbered." He was right. Strength begets strength.

The following year I quit drinking. I went to a hypnotherapist for support to do so. Quitting drinking was the easiest thing yet. The strength I gained from quitting smoking and ending the relationship seemed to have multiplied exponentially the amount of strength available to me. When I quit drinking, the physical rewards were wonderful. I had energy, my mind was clear, and I felt younger and healthier. Because I wasn't drinking, I went to bed earlier. Because I wasn't hung over, I got up earlier. My body literally bounced back to health. It was amazingly resilient, despite my years of abuse.

Now I am sixty-six. I have not smoked for fourteen years, and I have not had alcohol in thirteen years. My body is healthy and strong. I have a new relationship with my body because I am grateful that despite my former abuses, it still works. Now I know that I am responsible for it. I honor myself now by taking good care of my body.

Meanwhile, and through all this, I have grown really attached to my butterfly tattoo. My "mistake" seemed to me to be a sign of rebirth, given to me before I was even aware of the need. I took a good look at it the other day. I am so used to my butterfly's presence I often forget about it, reminded only occasionally when seeing the startled face of a mammogram technician who sees it for the first time. The sign of age, the drag of gravity, has now reached my butterfly. Neither my butterfly nor I am uncomfortable with our bodies changing. I get shorter and heavier with age, and my butterfly gets longer and thinner. All is well.

YOUR TURN

Discussion Questions:

1. Describe your body as it is today. What do you like about it? What would you change if you could?
2. In what ways do you abuse or neglect your body? In what ways do you respect and nurture yourself?
3. What constitutes good health to you? Has your view changed over the years? How does your lifestyle today support or not support your belief in what contributes to good health?
4. What do you fear about the effects of aging on your body? Have you come to terms with it? Why or why not?
5. Have you had an experience that created a radical change in your view of your body or health? If so, what was it? ? Why did it cause you to change?

Individual Exercise: *Face a Fear*

1. Write down five fears about your body or health.
2. Commit to face one of these fears. Then choose a date by which you will face the fear and the method you will use to do so.
3. Ask a friend to support you with this challenge. Then just do it!

Group Exercise: *Our Health Concerns*

1. Divide into two groups.
2. Each group will discuss and reach consensus about the most important health issues they are facing.
3. Each group will discuss and then declare
   - Five measures they are willing to take to stay healthy.
   - To what degree, expressed as percentage, they believe their health is in their hands.
4. Reconvene the group as a whole. A representative from each group will report its conclusions.
5. Compare the two groups' responses. How are they alike? How are they different?

Assignment:

Pretend you are the fourth author of *Saving the Best for Last* and write your story about "Accepting My Body" in your notebook.

Sexuality and the Big Five-Oh!

Some people might be wondering why we've included a chapter on sexuality. We've included it for the same reason we've included all the others: It's *important* for women over the age of fifty. Whether we have life partners or not, whether we are having sex or not, whether we have any interest in sex or not, our *sexuality* is important. We are sexual beings, and that means more than the act of having sex.

Our sexuality is part of us. It defines us as women. Our sexual journeys are important because they have shaped the women we are now and because our sexual history means so much more than what goes on between the sheets. Our sexuality includes not only the desire for sex but also the way we walk, the way we talk, the way we look at the world. We can flirt with men or with babies or with dogs. Without a direct object, we can flirt with the world.

Along with sexuality is passion. We all acknowledge that we can experience passion in the sexual act. Beyond that, we can take our passion into every other aspect of our lives. We can find passion in the everyday stuff of life or passion in global pursuits. We can be passionate beings without engaging in sex.

So, for those of you who are amused to see this chapter, or who believe it must be the shortest chapter in the book, boy have we got a surprise for you.

RENEE

For over two decades, I refused to take responsibility for my own sexuality. My sexual excitement came as a result of having things done *to* me. My fantasies all involved submission. To me, my sex life was full, frequent, creative. However, I did not fully realize that I wasn't an active participant.

I was married to the only man with whom I had ever experienced sex. He was in charge of our sex lives, just as he was in charge of our finances. He loved sex, and he loved me as a sexual partner. As long as I made him happy, there was no reason to question my sexual health.

Until age nineteen, I had done as my mother taught me. I stayed a virgin, if not until marriage, at least until I found a man whose desire to have sex with me was an act of love and not an act of conquest. I attributed my lack of sexual experience as a commitment to being a "good girl." I had survived the free love 1960s with my hymen and reputation intact. For years, I was smug about my adherence to a higher moral standard than what I saw swirling around me. The truth was I was afraid of boys and afraid of sex.

My husband was the first boy I had ever met with whom I was comfortable. As soon as I became comfortable, I felt free enough to let myself go in the sexual department. I relaxed and simply followed his lead. His lead lasted for over twenty years.

In my forties, my marriage began to unravel in a serious way and with it the standard of behavior that I had followed. In spite of any problems we had, my husband still wanted our sex lives to continue as usual, and so I continued to go along. He set the stage, and I played my role. It never occurred to me to do otherwise.

I wanted out of my marriage, but the reality of leaving was terrifying to me. Instead, I entered an emotional "anything goes" zone. If I couldn't physically leave, I could at least participate in activities that were outside the confines of what I considered acceptable for a happily married person.

I know now that the sexual decisions I made at that time were mistakes. I engaged in behaviors in opposition to the person whom I wanted to be. I was unfaithful, and my desires became the focus of my life. My marriage quickly dissolved.

Years later I realized that a good part of the sexual issues in my marriage were in large part due to the underlying issues with our relationship. If my husband's actions angered or frustrated me during the day, I couldn't be sexually open and vulnerable with him at night.

Although my choice to be unfaithful was a mistake, it did allow me to discover what sex could be like with a partner whom I trusted. I discovered that I was a complete sexual being, and that although another person could certainly ignite my sexual passion, I was just as capable of igniting someone else's.

I also discovered that my receiving pleasure was only part of the sexual process. The most powerful part was my using sex as a vehicle for honoring and adoring another human being. I had just started on my road to sexual maturity.

By my fifties, I went a step further. I got that the rules I had in my head were no longer serving me. Being a mature adult in society meant more than following rules. It meant having an internal moral compass that guided me.

I had never thought about that with regard to sex. It was an incredible thought that my sexuality was totally in my control and that whatever "rules" I followed would be created by me alone. If I chose, I could enjoy sex without being in love. If I chose, I could give sex without expecting a commitment. If I chose, I could use sex as a way to communicate my deepest feelings about my partner. I could choose to trust my sexual partner. Most importantly, I could choose to trust myself. And the deeper the trust, the more exciting and rewarding would be the sex.

I have never looked back. I continue to grow and my sex life continues to evolve. I have been blessed with sex partners who have readily expressed their enthusiasm for their experiences with me. Since turning fifty, I have heard men describe me as "sexy" far more often than I ever heard in my twenties.

Whatever their words say, I hear something at a deeper level. I hear their reaction to a woman who is completely comfortable with her sexuality. I hear their reaction to a woman who owns every second of what happens both in bed and out of it.

The best thing that came out of my awareness was that I internalized that I was sexy whether I was dating or not. I was sexy whether I had a sex partner or not. I was sexy because I knew that if my next sexual experience were the following day or years away, I was absolutely sure of one thing: I would have satisfying sex.

I am now in a relationship that is healthy, loving, giving, exciting. I am free to express my love for my partner through my sexuality. What happens between us in bed is a physical extension of what happens between us out of bed. As our relationship deepens, I am able to reach increasingly higher levels of sexuality with him. And just as I choose to impose no limits to our relationship in general, I choose to impose no limits to our levels of sexuality.

JOYCE

I am a survivor of incest that started when I was a young child. My father abused me until I was well into my teens. The abuse colored every relationship in my life. It poisoned my sense of self. It took my confidence, it made me feel less than whole, it made me feel different and abnormal. I grew up to become an angry woman, bitter and filled with hatred for my father and men in general.

My husband was the first man I chose to be with sexually. I loved him. He was a good, decent man. I was sexually excited by him. When we first married, he was gentle and understanding about my traumatic childhood. I loved the physical closeness, being touched, adored, and aroused. I didn't have orgasms, and so I faked them at first.

Whenever we argued, I repeatedly said that I didn't need him and never would. I could take care of myself. I was not conscious that this belief had a profound effect on my inability to experience orgasms and held me back from complete surrender and abandon with my husband. Over the years of our marriage, he began to lose patience with me. He could not understand or forgive my inability to have an orgasm with him. Since he did everything he could to understand me and to pleasure me, this meant that there was something wrong with me. He saw it as a slam against him. He called me frigid.

His reaction to me merely confirmed what I believed: I was abnormal and men were not to be trusted. My marriage ended.

During my thirties, I went into therapy for the first time. And I fell in love with a woman. My involvement in the feminist movement and friendships with straight and lesbian woman led me to believe women would be different from men as lovers, and that I would be able to trust and surrender.

For a while, the relationship worked. Then, of course, it didn't, because I wasn't any different. I did not trust men. I did not trust women. And I still wasn't able to understand what was stopping me from staying in a relationship. I was insecure, needy, and placing responsibility for unworkable relationships outside myself. I continued to experience life as a victim. I knew somehow my problems with trust and intimacy were linked to my father, and so I blamed my inability to trust on him.

I continued therapy into my forties. I dredged up the memories I didn't want to remember and relived them from the distance of years and maturity. Through hypnosis, I was able to recall the defining belief that ruled all of my relationships. When I was three years old, standing alone in a room, arms crossed defiantly across my small chest, I declared that I would never need anyone, never depend on anyone, never trust anyone. In the intervening years, that one room grew to become the entire world; but, I now saw that every single moment that followed in my life was exactly as my three-year-old self had intended it to be: separate, untrusting, alone. Arms crossed against the world.

I never knew or understood the depth, the implications of my childhood declaration. I never understood that my overwhelming desire to be tough was a barrier to the very thing that I craved in my life: emotional intimacy with another human being. So the realization was there, but I still had no way to obtain what I wanted.

After a second round of therapy in my forties, I went back to men. I had many affairs with men I knew and liked. I had a lot of sexual fun. I had no intimacy. I was still closed to creating what I wanted most. The three-year-old still stood in the room alone, arms crossed, defiant.

After all the affairs, I stopped dating for nearly ten years. I told myself that my work was fulfilling. My close friendships and loving family were enough. I didn't need a man to fulfill or complete me. I was resigned.

During my fifties, I participated in a series of workshops to do intensive self-exploration. The workshops gave me opportunities to work with myself and to see myself in relationship to others. This experience changed the way I looked at life and how I wanted to live. I was finally able to admit to myself and others that I would love to grow old with a partner.

My years in therapy had never taken away my fear of surrendering to a lover. I still had not experienced trusting a man, and I finally understood there was nothing to "learn" that would make that happen. Trusting someone is a choice.

At the age of fifty-six, I met a man at a dance. We connected, we dated, there was the possibility of sex. More than that, I saw the possibility of a long-term relationship. For the first time in my life, I really got that there would be no way for me to have a fulfilling relationship, sexual or otherwise, unless I was willing to trust. And so I made the conscious decision to trust. For the first time in my life, a door opened, leading me out of the room my three-year-old self had inhabited.

When I left that room, I was able to experience sexual intimacy, real sexual orgasmic intimacy for the first time in my life. It was a joyful, open, trusting, freeing intimacy. My three-year-old self had made a decision that allowed me to survive; now, my adult self had lifted the burden from her. I choose to remain open and trusting, to uncross my arms totally and completely.

The path to trust and intimacy was a long struggle over most of my adult life. I know that intimacy did not exist for me until that moment of choice and action. I did not know the true depth of what I was missing until I had it. And knowing I had it, I also knew that it wouldn't leave. Knowing I created it gives me great peace.

I am so grateful that I've had the opportunity to experience intimacy. I know it can happen again. I can choose to trust again, and again, and again.

JEAN

In the 1960s and 1970s, the world was having a great time in bed, or so it seemed to me. I was not. What should have been the simplest act, the most natural act, the act that Adam and Eve had no trouble with, was to me loaded with trouble and peril. I did not experience sexual passion.

I am still loath to share this truth with anyone because I know my image in the world does not match my reality. My image is I am strong, self-confident, energetic, and funny; the reality in the bedroom is I am needy, insecure, low-energy, and certainly not funny. I have been reluctant to reveal that to others or to myself. It embarrasses me. How can I be "living large" when I am a total wimp in the bedroom? I equate my inability to experience sex as others do as a failure. I see my friends as highly sexual, but I see myself as undersexed. I'm ashamed of that and so avoid sexual encounters.

My idea of what "should" be, what I "should" feel was formed in large part by the love comics I so adored in the early 1950s. In the love comics, the woman was always "carried away" by her own passion or the passion of others. In my fantasies, I am always carried away by passion. And that is what I want. I want to be swept away by physical passion. I want to forget myself, to surrender to the feelings of the moment. I listen to women friends talk about the passion of sex and the abandon, intensity, and pleasure they experience. I envy them that experience. I do not have it.

I sometimes thought that maybe my lack of passion wasn't so unusual and that maybe other women experience it also. But how would I know, since I have never shared this information with anyone.

Like many girls who grew up in the 1940s and 1950s, I was a virgin when I married. I had never seen a man naked and never experienced orgasm. Orgasm happened, almost by accident, on my wedding night, which I suppose was a damn good thing, because otherwise I wouldn't have seen any reason to continue what I experienced as basically stupid behavior. I do remember wondering why I didn't know about this stunning sensation before. I wondered why nothing had triggered the desire to explore; why nothing had happened, even accidentally, to create an urge for an orgasm before that moment.

So, my frustration with sex has nothing to do with orgasms, having or not having them. They can be created by me and by others (although self is more efficient about it). The culmination of sex is a biological event that can be produced. That is very different from passion. What I am missing is the passion: the attraction that builds internally to the demand for sex.

Here is what happens to me at the critical times: I don't know what to do with my racing brain when I am in bed with someone.

What do others do with their brains? Leave them in the car? Hang them in the closet? Put them in the pockets of their robes? How I would love to have somewhere to park my brain for a while. My experience, however, is that the damn brain is with me all the way.

I knew that my overactive brain had nothing to do with my choice of partners. Who and how they were being made no difference to how I was being. I could have Tom Cruise in bed with me and it would result only in my brain racing faster than ever. Nor is my racing-in-high-gear brain the result of the setting. Relaxed, tense, adored, at the beach, by candlelight, in the back seat of the car, on silk sheets, at my home, at his apartment. No difference. In love, in lust, in quest of sensation. No difference. The brain reigns supreme.

Although it seems a contradiction, even to me, I do love the intimacy of sex and the casual, intimate touch of a lover. I love the body contact, the implicit permission given for caresses, the thrill of being desired, and the sensuousness of connecting completely with another person. Yet I hear friends say, "We were so turned on we never made it to the bedroom," or "Just looking at him has me tremendously excited." That's the passion I have never experienced; and, if I haven't experienced it, then I am less than the whole woman I want to be.

Yet, I am a passionate person. I am passionate for justice, for my family, for the causes of women, for racial fairness, and for peace. I am passionate for dance, and I am passionate for fun.

So, what's up? Where's the sexual passion? There were some clues when I finally looked for them.

I am, by nature, a controller. Sexual passion is, by definition, "out of control." It is allowing your emotions and hormones to overrule your reason. Whew. I sweat thinking about it. But a deeper question is why do I need to control what happens in bed? What could happen if I was not in control?

Second, I am exceedingly self-conscious about my unclothed body. And really, this has little to do with the aging process. I had these same fears and inhibitions and opinions when I was twenty-five, thirty-five and forty-five. Age has simply added fodder to the already existing insecurity. I don't have a secret humpback. I just have very saggy breasts, a soft belly, big hips, and a mid-section that sort of collapses when I sit. But knowing I am insecure about my unclothed body doesn't answer why I am insecure about it.

I think I now know the answer to the brain in overdrive, to the need to control, to the over-concern about exposing my body. The answer has come through thought, prayer, writing, tears, coaching, conversations with myself, and conversations with my friends.

I was sexually molested as a child by a trusted figure—the friendly old elementary school janitor. I told no one at the time. After the abuse incident, he would come into my class to fix things, and would brush his hand across the back of my neck as he went by my desk. I would be frozen with fear and humiliation. I was totally, completely powerless. And I was ashamed.

I went all the way into my fifties, though, thinking that the abuse was not a big deal. After all, it was just one time, and many people had much worse things happen to them. When I was fifty-four, I was asked who in my life had betrayed my trust. It all came flooding back. I could feel him caressing the back of my neck—the neck I had never been able to bear any man touching sexually. I knew then that what had happened to me as a child had not been dealt with, and was still affecting my life.

I've been thinking and worrying about all this for a long time now. For the last several years, I have gotten to know myself better and better, but have not actively pursued sexual intimacy. It was the final frontier, and I just didn't even know that I wanted to try to cross it, only to try again, and fail again. . I did not want to put myself or anyone else through it again.

Well, that is over. Resignation really doesn't work very well as a lifestyle. I haven't solved this whole riddle for myself, but here is the work I've done so far.

I think my first conscious experience of sex taught me that sex was wrong, an occasion for shame, and that I couldn't trust men. Eventually, another child reported the molester. When I was ten years old, I had to testify in open court about exactly what he did to me. My parents were not allowed in the courtroom. No women were in the courtroom. My mother and father did the right thing, and the justice system did the right thing, but I was again horrified and humiliated.

All right, so now I know the source. And now, finally, it is time to deal with it. Time to take action, even through fear and dread.

The first thing I did was to have imagined conversations about the incident with everyone involved, especially the abuser. I spoke out loud. A dear friend taught me this method of reaching into painful areas. I asked the abuser why he did what he did and why he would do that to me. His answer came through my own lips: "I'm so sorry. I didn't mean to hurt you. I just couldn't help myself. I was a sick soul."

The only way I knew to change the situation was to forgive him. I even wanted to forgive him because I could see what a pitiful creature of God he was. And forgiving him let me assert some control, and let me decide how that incident would ultimately resolve.

Then I had another imaginary conversation. It was between a sex partner and me: "I am afraid that when I get undressed you will secretly laugh at my body. You will be judging it, and be horrified. It doesn't matter what reassuring thing you say to me about my body. I won't believe you."

When I then took the role of my sex partner, I was amazed at what came out of my mouth in response: "I really don't care what your body looks like. It would be an added benefit if your body were great, but so what if it isn't? We're here because I am attracted to you—to Jean—to all the qualities that make you, you."

"Oh. I never thought of that."

I am tired of allowing an event from childhood to control the sexual aspect of my life. I am tired of disappointing partners who expect a continuation of the person they knew, only to get a big baby in the bedroom. I regret that I allowed this situation to remain, even after I reinvented and created myself in virtually every other arena.

I'm not taking "no" for an answer any more. I think I have begun to see the forces that brought me to where I am and have begun to address them. I am committed to change and the real pursuit of passion in all areas of my life. I am working to understand the connections between my past and my present, and to change the behaviors resulting from those connections.

I will have passion.

YOUR TURN
Discussion Questions:

1. Have your beliefs about sex changed as you've aged? If so, in what ways?
2. Is sex more or less enjoyable for you at this time in your life? Why?
3. What is the difference between sex and passion? Can you have one without the other? Can you have passion in your life without any sex at all? Do you think it is possible to have a fulfilled, powerful life without sex? Explain.
4. Have you ever been molested or sexually abused? If so, how did it affect you? Does it continue to affect you? Does it affect your intimate relationships? What have you done about it? How have you coped?

Individual Exercises:
Exercise One: *It's All About Me*

In your notebook write the following: If I were solely responsible for my sexual pleasure and satisfaction, what would sex be like? What would I do to create what I want? How would sex be different from how it is now?

Exercise Two: *Perspective*

This is a very powerful exercise that can help you examine and release traumatic events, including sexual abuse. The intent of this exercise is to put to rest the hurt you experienced as a child. That way you can make room for you, as an adult, to live freely, no longer a victim. However, it may take more than this exercise to put your past behind you.

If you are doing this exercise alone and feel overwhelmed or anxious, just stop. You can start again at another time if you like. It is entirely up to you. If you think the exercise might be emotionally difficult for you, invite a trusted friend to sit with you throughout it. Your friend's role is just to be there as your security blanket.

1. Set aside a minimum of an hour for this exercise. Go to a safe, private space where you will not be interrupted. Take several pieces of paper and a fireproof container.
2. On each piece of paper, write the name of a person who played a role in your traumatic experience. Their role may have been

35

active or passive. It certainly would include you and the molester, but might also include your mother, the police, your friends, etc. "Played a role" may mean that someone didn't do what you thought he or she should do, or didn't notice that something was wrong. If you are holding onto grief, disappointment, or anger with someone, definitely put their names on pieces of paper. Limit yourself to five names.

3. Pick up the paper with your name on it. Speak out loud as yourself. Describe what happened to you. State how you feel about what happened to you. State whom you are angry with, whom you were disappointed in, and whom you are ashamed of (including yourself). Don't think. Just speak. Then set your piece of paper aside.

4. Pick up the abuser's paper. Speak for the abuser as if you were that person. Speak in the first person. Use "I" and "me." Say what he (or she) would tell you *now* if you asked him why he did what he did to you. Speak it out loud. Say whatever comes to mind without censoring it. It doesn't matter whether it makes sense. Be the person and speak aloud. Remember, you are not being you. You are being the abuser. When you are finished, burn that piece of paper.

5. One by one, speak for each participant in your drama. After each, burn her/his paper. The burning is a symbol that you are putting to rest your issues with that person.

6. Last, pick up your own piece of paper again. Now, with the experience of being each of the others, speak for yourself again. Say whatever last words you want to say to each of the participants. Forgive yourself for any part you thought you played in your abuse. Forgive all others. Burn your piece of paper.

7. Rest, take a bubble bath, breathe deeply. You've done good work. And remember, you always have the option of seeking professional assistance.

Group Exercise: *It's About Passion*

You will need a timekeeper for this exercise.

1. Choose a partner. Name a Partner A and a Partner B.

2. Partner A: Describe the one thing in life you love. Maybe it

is your artistic pursuits, family, a political or social cause, or a pet. Just be sure you choose something about which you are passionate. You have one minute to describe your passion, how you feel when you think about it, how you feel when you see it, or engage in it. Partner B will write the words and phrases you use when describing your passion.

3. Partner A: Take the list from Partner B. In one minute, describe your sexuality. In doing so, use as many of the words from your "passion" list as possible.

4. Switch roles and have Partner B describe her passion while Partner A takes notes.

5. After Partner B completes by talking about her sexuality using the words from her "passion" list, discuss with each other why (or why not) your passion shows up in your sexuality. If your experience of sexuality is not passionate, what would it take from you to have it be passionate? How would it change your experience? Does this discussion make you feel uncomfortable? Why?

Assignment:

Pretend you are the fourth author of *Saving the Best for Last* and write your story about "Sexuality and the Big Five-Oh" in your notebook.

Dating and Mating

If we followed the conventional path in life, we dated, and eventually we mated. If we were lucky (or in some cases, overcome by inertia), we never had to go through that process again.

But, decades later, many of us find ourselves single as the result of divorce or widowhood, emotionally back to the agonizing years of our early teens. We feel like we are standing at lunchroom or church dances, lined up at one end of the room with the rest of the girls, silently praying that a boy would ask us to dance, terrified that it actually might happen.

Now, though, we carry the emotional baggage of failed marriage(s) and relationships, or loss of a loved one through death or divorce. Whether through default or conscious choosing, some of us have always been single. No matter the cause, in our fifties and beyond, we still crave intimacy and companionship.

We also discover that in our absence, the dating scene is now fraught with new concerns. In our youth, the worst we remember are dire stories about the dangers of becoming pregnant. AIDS and HIV were, like global warming and killer bees, dangers unheard of in those relatively innocent times. Now, we are released into far more dangerous territory than unwanted pregnancy. We wrestle with, on the one hand, many years of post-virginal sexual experience and on the other, a feeling that we are mere moments beyond the onset of adolescence.

Many of us are less concerned with the creation of a new relationship than with how to even start the process again. Unlike the first time around, we no longer exist in the hormonal soup of high school or college. The opposite sex is no longer passing us in hallways, eyeing us at dances, sitting near us in classes. For many of us, our lives have settled into a daily routine of female friends, jobs, grocery shopping, and socializing with family and other couples. Aside from the myth of meeting the tall, handsome stranger who is fondling the rutabaga next to us at the local supermarket, we have no access to available men. Or so it seems.

While many aspects of dating may still be intimidating to older women, if we pause, relax and concentrate more on our strengths, we have the ability to come from a different place than we did all those years ago. Most of us see ourselves as being more focused, more self-aware, and less affected with societal expectations. We are less concerned with a man's looks, his wallet, or how many words are on his business card. We seek, instead, someone with common values and interests, intelligence, and a compatible personality. And, when bearing and raising children is no longer an issue, we have the luxury of creating relationships in which we have more energy to devote to our partners.

We three, like most people at midlife and beyond, still desire emotional and physical intimacy with others. And, like most people, our paths have not always been straight and true. We have made choices that didn't serve us, and we have changed our understanding of ourselves in the process. We have experienced success and failure. We have experienced growth and doubt. Above all, we have experienced.

RENEE

Intrigued by the original "speed dating" company begun by a rabbi in 2000, my friend Susan and I started a company called Brief Encounters. We were the first non-denominational speed dating company in the U.S., and we originally geared the events toward single adults over age forty. Because Susan and I were ourselves divorced and over age fifty, we were well aware of the challenges facing single mid-life daters.

A speed dating event brings equal numbers of age-compatible men and women together at a restaurant. Couples sit at individual tables facing each other. Each couple has a set number of minutes (anywhere from three to six) to talk to each other. At the end of each round, the men rotate to the next table and converse with their next partner. By the end of the evening, all men and women have had the opportunity to have their "mini-dates." Participants indicate on pre-printed sheets which people they would like further contact with. At the end of the evening, all sheets are tallied and mutual selections identified. Participants are then sent emails with the first names of their matches and contact information.

During the three and a half years we ran the company, we led about four hundred events and spoke to thousands of single adults. In the process, we learned as much about ourselves as we did about the participants. The following are some of the highlights.

Here are some beliefs that I have discovered to be untrue.

1. *It's impossible to know someone in just a few minutes.*

Impressions are made in ninety seconds. That's enough time for someone to ascertain demeanor, body image, and possible chemistry. Whatever time follows builds on that foundation.

2. *There aren't enough older men to go around.*

Contrary to public opinion, there *are* enough men in terms of sheer numbers. Though it may seem that they have relocated to another planet, it's just that they are not always so visible. Men of all ages are not as proactive as women when looking for a relationship. They would prefer to sit at home watching ESPN with a remote in one hand and a Michelob in the other, truly believing that their pizza delivery person will be a twenty-something five foot seven blond. This syndrome becomes more pronounced as men age, with the exception that even the appearance of the hot, young delivery girl may not be enough to get them into action.

Women are natural social networkers. We seek out other women for amusement, for support, for advice, and for no reason in particular. We are more apt to join clubs, form groups, attend meetings, and organize. When we are single, we are more likely to search out the kinds of activities that we hope will result in our meeting eligible men. Men are more work-related networkers. They are far less likely to feel the need to be in situations that involve face-to-face communication. Most men are comfortable attending sports events, not social mixers.

3. *Older men prefer younger women.*

Absolutely. On paper. *Not* so in person. Men are visual. Many men will voice opinions about women and age: "I like younger women," "Women my age look too old and/or are too sedentary," and "I only date women up to age (whatever)." Yet, when we took those same men and placed them in a room with real live women their age, strange things began to happen. They began to react favorably to the flesh-and-blood women they saw, without regard to an age label.

Often, men will be drawn to women older than them. I've heard lots of stories from women who are in relationships with much younger men, men who in theory wouldn't have thought they'd end up with a woman who was ten to fifteen years older than they are. But when they met face to face, the attraction was there.

Here are some secrets I've learned from a majority of men I've talked to:

- Men do not like cats;

- Men do not like to be questioned about what kind of car they drive, how much they make, or what on earth they do with their time now that they are retired;

- Men don't want to hear how your ex screwed you over, or how all men are slugs;

- Men don't want to know that you are still struggling to get over your last relationship.

I have also discovered the top three most important secrets about any successful encounter with any person that takes place in any situation, whether it be a speed dating event, a singles dance, a fix up, a coffee date at Starbucks, or a chance encounter at the dry cleaners:

- *Be in the moment.* Focus on the person you are talking to and not on yourself. Have the goal be to make whatever amount of time you have with them be valuable;

- *Know that you have absolutely nothing to lose and a lot to gain.* And I'm not just talking about potential love. I'm talking about learning more about yourself and how you relate to the world;

- And finally, *remember to breathe.* Your body language will be more inviting. Your speech will be more relaxed. Your breasts will be more prominent. (And the person facing you won't be called upon to perform an emergency lifesaving procedure on you.)

We all have preconceived notions about ourselves and others. Very often, these set-in-stone beliefs get in the way of meaningful connection with another human being. And they prevent us from being "in the moment" when we meet someone new. Let's face it, if you are thinking about your appearance or what you are going to say to someone, you are not listening to the other person. In other words, you are not present to the conversation.

Likeability has little to do with how you look but a lot to do with how you make people feel. Most people, when starting a conversation, have two things in mind: either to be engaging, funny, witty, and charming; or, to amass as much vital information about a person as possible. How would it be, if instead, your only goal was to find out what was really special about the other person? With that in mind, any encounter can be a great experience.

JOYCE

I never get enough sex. This is my little secret. Even though sexual intimacy was an issue for me until my fifties, I enjoyed the closeness, the passion, and the pleasuring of each other's bodies. Whenever I was having enjoyable sex, I wanted more. This is still as true for me now at sixty-six as it was when I was forty. I am still easily aroused and sexually responsive.

At fifty-six, I was not looking for a man. All I wanted to do was dance. My girlfriends and I went to our first singles dance for people over forty, and I met Andy. We dated for several months before we ever made love because I have always wanted to know my partner and feel a connection or chemistry before taking the plunge.

These days I have another rule about who I sleep with. I want to know a potential partner's sexual history and habits. I engage him in frank conversation about the necessity for taking precautions in this age of AIDS and other sexually transmitted diseases. After working for over fifteen years in the field of HIV/AIDS and knowing that seniors are contracting HIV-infection at one of the fastest growing rates in the U.S., I take STDs very seriously. I am not one of those people who think it can't happen to me. I've heard too many tragic stories from people who thought that. Thus, I require a certificate of health, meaning each of us must have an HIV test before I will go to bed with him.

Highly sexed and vibrant, women over fifty can be as sexually active as we ever were if . . . If we find an engaging partner. If each of us is healthy. If we know our own and his (or her) HIV status. If we practice safer sex by using condoms. So many ifs. At any age this is true, but being over fifty seems to bring its own challenges, its own "ifs." And I would say one of the big ifs is if...he doesn't have "dick flop"—as one of my acquaintances so delicately put it.

Many men our age are dealing with diminished libido and/or erectile dysfunction stemming directly from a drop in testosterone. The deluge of Viagra commercials tell us the problem is common. Drops in testosterone may also cause men to experience temporary impotence problems. They may not be as easily aroused, may not be able to respond as readily as they like, or their female partner may have to go to extra lengths to engage them.

The man I dated for the past five years was "Mr. Right" in the sex department. We were attracted to each other almost immediately upon meeting. As we dated and got to know each other, I liked the way we constantly touched and how aroused I felt when we held hands or kissed. The first time we made love was a joyous surprise: he was passionate, focused on my pleasure, patient, and his stamina allowed him to make love for hours. He was an accomplished, masterful lover.

I couldn't believe that at fifty-six I had finally met someone with the same sexual temperament as mine, someone as lusting and exuberant in bed as I wanted. It was almost too good to be true. We were very compatible, and my experience with him was free, spontaneous, accepting, and fulfilling. Feeling so sexy at my age was the *coup de grace*.

So I finally had the sexual partner of my dreams. But that was not the end of the story. After several years, my partner's testosterone level dropped so low, it became almost non-existent. He was not interested in sex the way he was when we met. After the doctor tested him and confirmed what we suspected, we agreed that medication was not a solution because of other health issues he was dealing with. It was something he and I openly discussed in order to deal with, and adjust to, our changing bodies and needs. We adjusted our expectations and adapted to his libido.

One of the most helpful adjustments involved planning for making love by planning a "sex date." That meant we assured he was rested, unstressed, and we did not wait until too late at night. We tried not to plan any other activities that would tire or distract us. Our facing the issue together and planning ways to support him contributed to a much more fulfilling and close relationship. It took the pressure off him to have to live up to unrealistic expectations and demands, and it made me more mindful of his needs. We continued to have a fulfilling sex life—it was just not as frequent as I would have liked.

I was horny sometimes, and I missed much of the spontaneity we had earlier in our relationship, but I chose to deal with what was a fact of life. I think the key to making this work for us was my attitude and my willingness to talk about it. By being supportive and patient, our sexual relationship was fulfilling and enjoyable for both of us.

Right now I am not in a relationship, yet I anticipate having great sex again. When and if…

JEAN

I am sixty-six years old. I've been complaining for a couple of years that there are NO men around to date. This assertion is met by a variety of responses. Younger women and all men say, "Oh sure there are." This is then followed by, "Maybe you are not looking hard enough." Women my age respond, "Isn't *that* the truth!

I decided to try a scientific approach to the question of whether there are men out there for women my age to date. First, I identified the subject population. I would consider dating men somewhere between fifty-five and seventy This seems a reasonable age range: older than my children and younger than my father. I fired up my computer and logged on to a major Internet dating service. The men listed on this dating service are not just a cross-section of all men; these are men who are straight and single and actively looking for someone to date.

I searched the dating service for men between fifty-five and seventy who lived fewer than one hundred miles from me. One hundred fifty-two men showed up. Hurray! This looked good.

Of the 152 men, only eight had any interest in dating any woman over sixty, and only one of the eight was interested in dating anyone over sixty-two. One man out of 152 would consider dating me. One hundred fifty-one men over fifty-five thought I was too old. I had no idea the ratio would be that terrible.

I was curious though about whom these 152 men did want to date. The answer was distressing. Over sixty percent wanted to date women under forty-five—a minimum of ten years younger than they were. Eight of them wanted women under thirty-five—twenty years younger than they were! Then there were the two dreamers who wanted to date women under age twenty-five. They themselves were fifty-five and fifty-seven years old. Surely they are living in fantasy heaven.

We women of a certain age are caught in a dilemma. If we want to be in a romantic relationship, the statistical evidence is that we have to look at men well older than we are. If you figure that the vast majority of men are looking for women ten to twenty years younger than they, that means I need to be looking for men who are between the ages of seventy-three and eighty-three. Oh my. If I were to believe only the statistics, I would believe there were no men interested in dating me.

But that's the computer. What about real life?

Because I love to dance, I regularly attend weekly dances for over-forty singles. There are usually about 150 women and about 200 men in attendance. The dances are from 7:00 p.m. to 11:00 p.m. (in honor of our advanced age).

The majority of the men are between fifty and seventy. They are nice men who are looking for women to date, perhaps fall in love with and marry, and they don't seem choosy about age. But many are overweight, out of shape, and physically lazy. Most are retired and seem to equate retiring from their jobs with retiring from life. They look and act old, tired, and dispirited.

While I don't doubt that these men would like to find romance and would consider women their own age, including me, the fact is that I am not attracted to them. I am looking for a partner for exploration, fun, dance, and life; not for a partner who is resigned to a half-life.

I think that there are men out there with whom I could become romantically linked, but they certainly are not plentiful. I think that the bounty of eligible, desirable men we took for granted when we were in our teens and twenties and thirties doesn't exist any more.

I could resign myself to a future without romantic involvement. That would not be the end of the world. I have lived many years without romantic involvement and have been very happy. In fact, my last ten years have been amazingly generative.

I choose to believe, however, that if a love partner is intended to show up, he will show up. He could appear in my life in connection with modeling, or with the workshops I give, or the civil rights consulting I do, or he could pop up out of my past. When I am engaged in activities I love, I am at my best and my most natural. I am relaxed and tuned in to the people with whom I am working. How lovely it would be to have a partnership created organically rather than mechanically.

I don't know where he will come from, and I don't need to know. My job is only to live my life, and should he appear, to be open and welcoming.

YOUR TURN
Discussion Questions:
1. What are the differences between dating after fifty and dating when we were younger? What do you look for now in a date or relationship? What is your experience in finding romantic partners? Is it easy or difficult?
2. If you are unmarried, are you open to the idea of marriage or a committed relationship? Why or why not?
3. Do you want or need intimacy (both sexual and non-sexual) in your life? Why or why not? What qualities do you bring to a relationship?
4. How, if at all, has the specter of AIDS or other sexually transmitted diseases affected your sexual behavior? Do you discuss these issues with your partner(s)?

Individual Exercises:
Exercise One: *A Great Date*
One fear of many women over fifty is venturing out on their own to a social event, yet going alone is the best way to meet new people—both men and women. When you go with a friend, the temptation is strong to stay together and just chat with each other. So, prepare to go on a date with yourself.

1. Look in your local newspaper or on the Internet for an event. It may be a dance, an art exhibit opening, a book signing, or whatever.
2. Sign up for it. If you have an issue about safety in traveling to the event alone, then prepare to splurge on a taxi.
3. Treat this as a special occasion: luxury bath, manicure, massage, whatever it takes to be very nice to yourself. Dress carefully—after all, you have a great date: YOU.
4. Go to the event with a clear agenda. Speak with at least three people you do not know, and leave with contact information, or a "date" with at least one of them. When you meet and talk with people, focus out. People will find your interest in them appealing. Forget yourself and learn about the other person. The purpose here is not to make a romantic connection (although wouldn't that be nice) but to practice making connections in a social situation.
5. When you get home, write your experience of your date with

yourself. What did you learn about yourself? Were you a good date? Are you willing to do this again?

Exercise Two: *Take It to a Ten*

You have the power to change a relationship by changing your attitude, behavior, and actions.

1. Write in your notebook the names of the ten most important people in your life, including family, friends, co-workers, boss, etc. Next to each name, write a number from one to ten that represents the quality of your relationship with each person on the list—with one being a terrible relationship and ten being a perfect relationship.

2. For each relationship under a five rating, think about what it would take for you to make the relationship a ten. Assume it is entirely in your power to improve the relationship. Commit to make at least one of these relationships become a ten within a week.

3. Contact the person you have chosen. Speak to that person from your heart, and explain your desire to have a "ten" relationship. Say how much you appreciate him/her, and why he or she is important in your life. If you believe you have offended or hurt this person, ask for forgiveness.

4. Write about this experience in your journal. What did you create? What did it take from you? What did you gain?

5. Enjoy the new relationship you have created.

Group Exercise: *Fast Friends*

The goal of this exercise is to understand that we can instantly create relationship with each other.

One person must serve as a timekeeper.

1. Arrange the chairs in two parallel rows with pairs of chairs facing each other. Note: If you have few people in the group, use a configuration that will work so that each person can speak to everyone. If you have a large group, you may wish to make two separate sets of lines.

2. Have each person choose a seat and face her partner.

3. You have three minutes to talk with the person in front of you. If the group is small, take five minutes for each person. Your only focus is the other person drawing her out, and making

this a great experience for her. You must not care what the person thinks of you. Remember, this is a conversation, *not* an interview. You aren't taking turns speaking.

4. The timekeeper will indicate when to start the conversation and when three minutes elapse.

5. When three minutes are up, the timekeeper will say, "Move." The people in only one of the lines will move one chair to the right. The person formerly in the end seat must come around to occupy the first seat. Everyone should now have a different partner.

6. Begin the next three-minute session. Repeat these three-minute sessions until everyone has talked to everyone else in the opposite line.

7. When the rotations are over, convene as a group and discuss your experience.

   - What did you learn about your partners? What did you learn about yourself?
   - Did you meet your goal of having each three minutes be a great experience for your partner?
   - How did you behave during each conversation? Did you always wait for the other person to speak? Did you always go first? Did you behave differently from person to person?
   - Did how you behaved in the exercise reflect how you behave in life? Is it working for you in you life?
   - Were these conversations different from the usual communications you have with people? Why or why not?
   - How did it feel to have your partners focus totally on you and care more about you than they did about themselves?
   - How was it when you stopped depending on another person to create an enjoyable experience for you but instead depended totally on yourself to create it?

Assignment:
Pretend you are the fourth author of *Saving the Best for Last* and write your story about "Dating and Mating" in your notebook.

Physical Surprises

After all the years we have spent looking into mirrors, why is it that we didn't have a clue what was going to happen to our bodies after age fifty? We received advance warning about the effects of puberty and childbirth, but nobody mentioned the changes that begin slowly around forty-five, and then pick up steam once the fifty barrier is crossed. Many of us thought pregnancy and childbirth provided the greatest changes in our bodies and that once our last child was born, our bodies wouldn't undergo anything as drastic.

We knew old people looked different than we did, but we thought it was just a matter of gray hair and wrinkles. How could we know that gray hair and wrinkles were just the final result of small disasters all along the path? And the really awful part was that most of the surprise changes that happened to our bodies could not be discussed in mixed company. No one wants to hear about body parts sagging, bagging, or dragging, or leaving town altogether; but it happens. Nobody wants to hear about exactly where, on your body, you lose your hair; but that happens, too.

And how about the fact that we get shorter as our spines compact? For some of us that's no great tragedy. Tall people have an inch or two to spare. For short people though, getting shorter can be a mean trick of fate. To make it worse, the shortening of our spine seems to coincide with the day we realize our stiletto heels can now only be used to smash bugs and not put on our feet. When we were young and broke a bone, did anyone tell us it would show up again at around age fifty as arthritis? When we had babies, did anyone tell us our internal muscles stretched much as our stomach muscles did and could start to give out around age fifty?

With all of the medical specialties in the world that seem to take us from cradle to grave, we think they missed one. We know from pediatricians about young bodies, and we know from gerontologists about old bodies. In between those two categories there are doctors for all kinds of conditions that might hit the adult body. We three authors think there are just too many physical surprises. We recommend a new medical specialty just for people over fifty. The specialty would educate us to *expect* not-so-subtle changes and not be frightened. The doctors, hopefully all women our age, would probably spend a lot of time holding our hands. And then we could all go out for pizza.

RENEE

Everybody talks about the fact that as we age, the human body becomes less efficient. My experience has been otherwise. My body is now automatically ejecting unnecessary parts!

It started a couple years ago, when I began to have a slight feeling of fullness in my vaginal area. When I stood in the shower, it was especially pronounced. After awhile, I could feel a bulge between my legs. My response was to push the bulge back and keep showering. Problem solved.

After about a year of those bodily gymnastics, I was sitting on the toilet one day and, suddenly, there seemed to be a very large SOMETHING sticking out of me.

Now, I have a confession to make. I've never really grasped the finer points of the functioning of the human body. I always disliked anything science-related in school. I even tried, as an adult, to look at those books where you flip transparent pages that take you deeper and deeper into the human body. I stopped when it was clear that I didn't possess a valid stamp in my passport for whatever territory I was entering.

I grew up in the era of "Babies are sent from heaven. Case closed." There was once a story in the local newspaper about a baby found in a mailbox. I asked my mother why anyone would want to get rid of a "gift from God." My mother explained that when women were married, babies were, indeed, a gift. When women weren't married, babies were a punishment. I spent the next couple years believing that shoplifting would lead straight to babies.

I counted on my elementary school to rescue me from my ignorant state. Each year, the seventh grade teacher showed a film to the girls of the class, entitled "You're A Young Lady Now." This was a film that was supposed to usher me into the mysteries of mature womanhood. In my school, the anticipation started in fifth grade, and built steadily until that magic moment when the boys would be unceremoniously kicked out so that we could see the film.

But, alas, several days before the film was to be shown, my teacher stood up in front of us and announced that she felt that our particular class was too immature to see the film. I was devastated, doomed to spend the rest of eternity never knowing the secrets of what was below my waist. I grieved for the loss of such knowledge, but I told myself that at whatever point in the future I would have children, all mysteries would be revealed. They weren't.

When I gave birth the first time, after forty-five hours of fairly hard labor, I was a wee bit too distracted by contraction-induced mental illness to focus on the overhead mirror that was provided. Subsequent births were mercifully so short that I barely had time to yell, "I hate everyone's guts!" before slippery little bodies shot into the doctor's hands.

In spite of all this, I developed my own theory that went something like this: Organs should stay inside of bodies; babies should come out. Clearly, anything that came out of that particular place in my body should have a face on it. That theory stood me in good stead until I turned fifty.

This brings us to that fateful morning when I was confronted with the SOMETHING coming out of me. A mirror between my legs informed me that the SOMETHING that was now highly visible DID NOT HAVE A FACE. So if it wasn't a newborn, then I was starting to eject body parts.

Calling upon all of the emotional reserves and maturity I possessed, I promptly became hysterical. I hobbled to the phone as fast as I could, keeping my legs tightly pressed together. Every few inches, I looked back to make sure there was not a liver or kidney lying on the floor.

The nurse at the doctor's office listened to my medically detailed explanation ("SOMETHING is falling out of my body!") and offered me an appointment a week in the future. The conversation went something like this:

"Hi, this is Renee Fisher. There is SOMETHING falling out of my body!"

"Are you a patient of the doctor's?"

"Yes, and there is SOMETHING falling OUT of my body!"

"Would you like to come in?"

"Yes, IMMEDIATELY. There is SOMETHING falling OUT OF MY BODY!"

"Okay, how about next week?"

"By next week, I will have no internal organs left. I will be empty. I need to come in NOW."

"Okay, tomorrow then."

"Okay, should I stay in bed with a bucket between my legs?"

"Not necessary."

"WHAT IS FALLING OUT OF ME?" Silently, I was negotiating with the universe. *I'll give you the appendix but not the colon. One kidney is expendable, one liver isn't.*

"I don't know, but the doctor will check you out."

The doctor did check me out and the verdict was a "prolapsed bowl."

"Why are things falling out of me?" I asked the doctor, feigning nonchalance.

"Well," the doctor said, "your ligaments got stretched out during childbirth."

"So did my nerves, but I got over it."

"Ah," the doctor said, "but you had a hysterectomy. Think of the uterus as a tent pole. When you removed it, the tent collapsed, along with everything around it." I've heard of bodies being temples. Mine was a campsite after a hurricane.

Suffice it to say that I survived the collapse of my internal organs. But I will never be blasé again about my body having the ability to contain its parts. And I was angry that in the hundreds of pages that I read to prepare me for childbirth, this was never mentioned. I never saw an article, a TV documentary, a segment on "60 Minutes", a doctor's office pamphlet relating to this not-uncommon problem. When I mentioned it to friends my age, they all understood. On the other hand, my twenty-four-year-old personal trainer at the gym had never heard of such a thing. She mentioned it to another trainer who told her I was making it up.

In my mother's generation, menstruation wasn't talked about openly. In my generation, menstruation came out of the closet, along with full color ads for tampons, mini pads, and over-the-counter meds to combat cramps. Now, in my daughter's generation, menopause has made its grand entry. We acknowledge the existence of hot flashes, memory loss, and irritability, along with dozens of books and hundreds of magazine articles.

The "closet" might be less full than it was, but there's still more crammed in there that's waiting to see the light of day. Personally, I'd like to see the issue of prolapse finally exposed before the actual *organs*.

JOYCE

As I looked in the mirror at my naked body this morning, I was reminded of my grandmother laughing and teasing me about the few strands of pubic hair that appeared on my *mons pubis* prior to adolescence. Today she would giggle for the opposite reason: my pubic hair is disappearing.

After I turned fifty, new things began appearing on my body while others disappeared from their usual abode. Moles and other skin growths proliferated, including "tags" on my neck like the ones my grandmother had. Hair made random appearances around my face, conspicuously on my upper lip, chin, and neck. And like my pubic hair, my eyebrows thinned and those remaining grew askew.

Body parts faded in color. My areola, the ring of color around the nipple of my breast, was now pale pink. My eyebrows got lighter, and my hair turned white.

Body parts went south, starting with my eyelids. Everything else followed, including my breasts, stomach, butt, and skin on my forearms. My jaws turned into jowls, my chin sagged, and I developed chicken neck. Even my earlobes drooped.

My body developed wrinkles, folds, and excess skin. Wrinkles appeared on my face, as folds of skin developed everywhere fat accumulated. Folds of skin hang over the back of my bra, like breasts on my back. Skin folds fall over my waistband no matter how much weight I lose, making it impossible to find my waist.

While body parts are traveling south, none have yet fallen out. I say "yet" because I am sure one organ is close. No longer supported by my uterus, my bladder has prolapsed. The symptoms are embarrassing and annoying. When I sneeze, cough, laugh too hard, or wait just a moment too long to go the bathroom, my bladder leaks. I go to the bathroom more frequently than ever in order to avoid a mishap, but my bladder never seems to be completely empty. Involuntary urination is unavoidable.

Although some of these changes may be inevitable, I think I really didn't expect them to happen to me. This disconnect is hard to explain. It may be due to outright denial. I feel young so how can these changes possibly be happening to me?

I had no idea that I would have to work so hard at taking care of my exterior. I use anti-aging creams, moisturizers, sun screen, color and style my hair, wax, shave, get weekly manicures and pedicures, apply makeup, and stay out of the sun. I learned new makeup techniques, including how to use softer colors and ways to camouflage flaws in my skin.

While I address the exterior challenges of aging, I also attend to the internal aspects of aging. I refuse to accept as inevitable the many problems that our culture associates with aging. I do not believe that because I grow older, I have to be frail, sick, or disabled. Diseases such as osteoporosis, muscle weakness, and high blood pressure are alleviated or preventable through proper nutrition, regular exercise, and getting enough sleep.

To stay healthy I stay mentally active, productive, and involved in challenging and stimulating work and social activities. I also nurture my soul through nature, prayer, and meditation. While I recognize that physical exercise is more important than ever, I still tend to procrastinate. It is always the last thing I want to do. When I exercise, I go for walks or use the treadmill. I never do it as often as I should. I am still struggling to make it a habit in my daily routine.

Physical changes may continue to surprise me, but I will not fight aging. I will love and accept myself as I am. I continue to nurture myself and keep up my appearance. I want to age in health and with grace.

JEAN

I've been through the women's movement. I've read *Our Bodies, Ourselves*. I thought I pretty much knew whatever I needed to know about the workings of the human body. I am, after all, an enlightened modern woman and have given birth to two children.

I got up one morning, and my uterus fell out. I did not know what was happening to me. I knew something was coming out, but I did not know *what* body part it was. Nothing actually fell on the floor, but it made it no less scary that something was coming from a place nothing was scheduled to come from, and trying, it seemed, to fall on the floor!

The emergency doctor on duty at my HMO replied to my frantic phone call by saying, "Huh...sounds like a prolapsed uterus. It's not an emergency." Apparently, having babies weakens the muscles that hold things in place (like your uterus, bladder, and other organs you don't want to think about). In about ten percent of women, most of them post-menopausal, the uterus falls down and reaches for the nearest exit. In extreme cases like mine, several body parts were competing to get out.

The nonchalance of the doctor unsettled me even more. Damn! How could something so surprising and so major be happening to me and be viewed as so common and minor in the medical profession?

And, if a falling uterus were not bad enough, worse was waiting. When I went screaming to my HMO gynecologist, he told me this condition was not considered pathology, but rather a natural happening, thus only one treatment was available for coverage. He handed me a hard rubber ring called a pessary, rather like a baby's teething ring, and told me to push it up my vagina to the cervix where it would hold my uterus inside of me. I was to wear this forever. The HMO would not approve any surgical remedy for my organs falling out.

I asked what I was to do with the lovely little ring should I have the desire and opportunity to have sexual relations. He blushed. He said I could take it out or leave it in. He didn't say how I should explain it to my partner. ("Listen, that hard thing you feel up there is a device to keep my organs in. Don't worry about it. Just enjoy yourself.") It was clear to me that the sex life of a woman over fifty was not only of no interest to this doctor, it actually embarrassed him to discuss it. And while I would like to say that I reacted in outrage, that I told him what I thought of him, the HMO, and the whole medical profession, the fact is that I sat silent. I felt embarrassed, and at that moment, I felt old, enfeebled, and invisible.

It took six months to get out of the HMO, during which time I wore sanitary pads and tight underwear to hold everything in. I then went to a female doctor in private practice. She was horrified at my treatment by the HMO and scheduled surgery immediately. I had a hysterectomy, and all other organs were sewn back into place.

I now talk to other women about subjects like falling uteri. I want to bring all of the physical body experiences of being women over fifty into the common conversation of women. I want the physical changes created by age to become normal, expected, and yes, even interesting. If it is up to me, there will be no surprises for my daughters and granddaughters and their friends. The jig is up. The secrets are leaking out.

YOUR TURN
Discussion Questions:
1. What physical surprises have you encountered since your forties? Since menopause? Since your fifties? Have you found talking with your doctor helpful? Why or why not? With whom, besides your doctor, have you discussed body changes? Where do you get the best information?
2. Do you have fears about how you are changing physically? If so, what are they?
3. There is a temptation to glorify the new-found energy of us post-fifty women, without also acknowledging the unexpected and largely unwelcome physical aspects. Should we be talking to our daughters and granddaughters about these age-related changes? Can we learn to appreciate, rather than to resist, these changes?

Individual Exercise: *Picture This*
1. Draw a picture of yourself on large poster board or sheet of paper. Mark on the picture areas of your body that have changed in the past few years due to the natural aging process.
2. Under each change, note whether:
   - You consider the change positive or negative and why.
   - You have revealed and talked about these changes with your mate and/or with women friends. Why or why not?
3. Do some healing work.
   - Talk to your body. Forgive yourself for the most natural thing in the world: aging.
   - Focus on getting the best information possible about any particular change, discussing it with friends and professionals if necessary,
   - Focus on creating and maintaining good health.

Group Exercise: *How Embarrassing!*
1. Find a partner. Choose a Partner A and a Partner B.
2. Select an age-related physical change to your body that embarrasses you so much you have not revealed it to anyone. Tell it to your partner. Talk about why it embarrasses you.
3. After you both have revealed your secrets, start laughing!

Assignment:
Pretend you are the fourth author of *Saving the Best for Last* and write your story about "Physical Surprises" in your notebook.

Weighing In

Children may grow up and leave. Husbands, jobs, finances may come and go. Residences, hair color, and bra size may change. Sometimes it seems that for many of us the only constant in our lives is the desire to lose weight.

What is it about weight that has so many women in turmoil? We blame the media for presenting us with an idealized role model of what a woman should look like: artificially inflated boobs perched atop a pin-thin frame. Yet, a casual stroll down any street in the country (save, perhaps Rodeo Drive in L.A.) will tell us that real women have normal size breasts and considerably more meat on their bones than women on TV and in the movies.

In spite of reality (real reality, not media reality), we believe that the loss of five or ten or one hundred pounds will improve our lives. While it's clear that some of us should lose weight for our physical well being, many of us spend years struggling to lose an amount of weight that doesn't impact on our health. Our rules about what we should weigh are often determined more by a standard we have set for ourselves, rather than one recommended by physicians.

Rather than go into the deep-seated reasons we are this way, we simply accept this as a fact of life. We drink diet Cokes with our pepperoni pizza. We hit the gym and go out for lunch after. We eat one cookie, decide our diet is blown and cheerfully consume the entire bag. We eat to celebrate, to mourn, to pass the time, to connect with others.

The passage of years doesn't help us. As we age, most of us find that the pounds go on more quickly and leave more reluctantly. They are obnoxious party guests who refuse to leave, in spite of our best efforts. The eating patterns we established when we were younger no longer work. The occasional slice of pizza seems to show up the next morning on the scale. And it seems that one day of fool-hearty consumption takes many days to correct.

At some point, we get to come to terms with all this. We get to shift from food as enemy to food as friend. The best we can do regarding food is to see it solely in terms of healthy versus non-healthy, rather than fat versus non-fat, and get off the scale for good. We three authors are seriously considering this notion and will discuss it further over non-fat mocha caramel frappuccino ice cream (one point).

RENEE

Coffee Häagen-Dazs does for me what alcohol does for others. It provides a profound sense of well being and joy, followed the morning after by angst and guilt. My reaction is to berate myself for being so weak-willed and inferior to all the people of the world who can calmly sit down and eat one scoop or one cone or one dish of ice cream and not feel it necessary to inhale the entire container.

Although this addiction followed me through most of my adulthood, it became increasingly more difficult to go on the wagon as the years went by. The common reaction to my telling people about my addiction was "Goodness, you are fifty! (or fifty-one or fifty-two....) Aren't you at the age where you should just be able to loosen up and enjoy yourself without worrying about anything?" The preceding argument had great validity, especially when I was staring at the familiar burgundy and white container with the picture of dark little coffee beans on the front. Joy was merely a spoon away (or a fork or a knife or a finger...)

Like many women my age, the same excess weight dogged me into its second decade as I approached fifty. Although I was indeed at an age when I should be able to loosen up and enjoy life without worrying about anything, in the realm of everything that was possible in my life, eating vats of ice cream seemed a bit insignificant as the definition of "loosen up and enjoy life."

So I made a change. Each year beginning with my fiftieth birthday, I would take on a new physical challenge, a new social challenge, and a new mental challenge. I loosened up and enjoyed myself in ways that did not require a utensil. I created a declaration that required commitment instead. Coffee Häagen-Dazs was around every corner. (Believe me, I know. I've checked out all the corners.) It's easy to get, relatively cheap, and perfectly legal. Coming up with satisfying alternatives was more difficult than I had considered.

I've made good on my promise to myself over the last ten years, and one result is that I no longer rush to the freezer with zealous regularity. Instead, I have walked hundreds of miles for breast cancer and on my treadmill, rafted down whitewater, and flown in a helicopter. I've had my writing published and started a new company. I've gone dancing and gone online and have met lots of men. I have highlighted my hair, had laser surgery and minor cosmetic surgery.

Importantly, although I joined a gym thirty years ago, it was only since turning fifty that I hired a personal trainer. I realized that on my own, I thought of excuses to go easy on the workouts or to skip them entirely. My regimen now includes two one-hour sessions per week with the trainer on machines, free weights, and abdominal exercises. I also try to walk two miles per day, five days per week on the treadmill. In addition to improving the exterior of my body, weight training helps ward off osteoporosis, a common outcome of my spinal disorder.

Best of all activities, I've discovered that increased sexual abandon involves my brain to such a degree that I totally forget about the existence of Häagen-Dazs . (Okay, sort of.)

I still go on occasionally indulge in coffee Häagen-Dazs, but it is no longer my mainstay. I do not believe I'll ever be a truly disciplined eater; but, I'm regularly eating fresh fish and salads for the first time in my life, and I limit my carbohydrate and sugar intake. I am not only more conscious of what I do with my body, but also with what I put into my body. In doing so, I've kept off that extra ten to fifteen pounds for several years now.

So as the aging process continues its relentless course, I feel like I'm still improving with each year. Aside from regular whining at my personal trainer, I'm enjoying it.

JOYCE

I am a thin woman in my not-so-thin body.

Most women I know have issues surrounding excess weight. All my life, I have heard women talk about their diets and complain *ad nauseum* about how fat they are. Not me I say. I felt some sympathy for my girlfriends, but I could not share their particular weight issues. I had the opposite problem. I was so thin my mother made me special milk shakes to try to put weight on me. When I graduated from high school, I was five feet five inches and weighed ninety-seven pounds.

By the end of my freshman year in college, I had happily put on thirty pounds. I delighted in gaining weight even as I outgrew all my clothes. Although I could not afford a new wardrobe, I was finally the perfect weight for my height. I learned to sew, made new clothes, and never again worried about being underweight.

All the way to my late forties, I enjoyed the luxury of eating anything and everything I wanted without upward fluctuations in my weight. Calories and quantity never mattered. An exercise program was totally unnecessary. The only time I was ever weight-conscious was when I was pregnant. The obstetrician warned about the dangers of gaining too much weight and how hard it would be to lose it after giving birth—not a problem.

Unlike many people who ate compulsively when stressed or depressed, I was the opposite. Being stressed was like being on a diet: I would lose weight. I could go for days without eating and never miss it. I lost weight whether I needed to or not.

My old bad habits that never used to matter became my downfall. In my fifties, I began to comfort and nurture myself through eating. More frequently than I care to admit, I grabbed a gallon of ice cream from the freezer, got a spoon, and plunked myself down to read a good book or play computer games. Calories and quantities began to matter.

I regretted the passing of an era when weight was not an issue. I was finally forced to monitor what I ate and, on top of that, to exercise. I had to be responsible. I had to be rigorous. I had to be consistent. It seemed too much like work. I wanted it to be easy like it was when I was under fifty. I wanted to throw a temper tantrum because my metabolism turned against me.

Now when I look in the mirror, I am surprised at how I look. Instead of seeing the thin person I am in my mind's eye, I see the real me with a flabby roll around my waist and my heavy thighs. My weight crept up, a pound or two a year, causing the carefree, diet-free life I knew to go away, along with my thin body.

I still have a little more weight to lose; but, more importantly, I am challenging myself to stick to a healthy diet to improve my overall health as well as to ward off re-gaining the weight. My exercise regimen is becoming routine (albeit slowly). I feel much more energetic and my clothes fit better. I like how I feel in my body, and I have a sense of well-being because I am taking care of myself.

JEAN

You know, I could deal with the fact that from now until I depart this earth I will be fighting the battle of the pudge, if the fight weren't so damn unfair. I have two major questions about weight: why *do* we start gaining weight after age fifty, and why doesn't it happen in the same way to men?

I have, my whole life, been tall and slim. In the seventh grade, my father oh so elegantly declared I was a "long drink of dirty water" (just the kind of attention certain to bolster seventh grade confidence). His iffy humor aside, the fact was that by the seventh grade I had reached my full height of five feet nine inches and weighed barely enough pounds to cover my bones. I was skinny with knobby knees and no shape.

Those characteristics became my friend in my twenties. I filled out nicely. I had an actual shape. It was around this time that some of my friends began to battle weight gain from having babies. Not me! I gained a total of only five pounds when pregnant with my first child, and maybe ten pounds with the second. My metabolism was an efficient system for dealing with any potential weight gain. I never worried about what I ate, and never exercised.

Then I hit fifty and my body pulled a sneak attack. Extra pounds started appearing on my body. What had happened? I wasn't eating more. I wasn't exercising less (or at all). But here came the pounds. What was with that? I mean, really! While my eating habits held steady, up went the weight. It began at maybe five pounds per year at first and was so gradual that it almost seemed not to matter.

When my weight got up to one hundred seventy pounds (from an average of one hundred forty-five pounds), I took a long look in the mirror. I realized I had stopped looking at my whole self in that mirror. For the previous year, not liking what was happening below my neck, I had been looking only at my face and ignoring all else. So now I looked. I saw my usual face, neck, arms, and upper body, but my lower half was looking grim. I could see why my waistbands were rolling down, buttons popping open, and seams straining. My waist had disappeared. I now was straight up and down except—well—except for the saddle bags and blooming butt. I had gone up three sizes and was pushing on to the next size. I had changed the way I dressed from tight jeans and slinky shirts to baggy pants and big shirts (the ones that cover your whole butt).

I went into emergency mode. Off I went to Jenny Craig. I became the perfect client, losing the predicted two pounds per week. It took me thirteen weeks to lose twenty-five pounds. That may not sound like much time until you think that thirteen weeks is more than three whole months of eating plastic food in portion sizes intended for five year-olds. It is ninety-one days of denying yourself the delicious tastes of chocolate, and cookies, and candy, and buttery popcorn, and rich French sauces, and pasta, and great breads.

I succeeded on that diet and went back to my safe 145 pounds. I kept the weight off for about a year, but it came back on again as I made an exception here and there to my healthy diet. And worse yet, the weight came back on faster than it had before. Now, on average, I was gaining seven to ten pounds a year.

I have repeated the "lose the weight, put it back on" cycle repeatedly since I turned fifty. I have done Jenny Craig twice, Weight Watchers twice, LA Weight Loss twice, and Dr. Atkins once. And guess what: they all work. I have repeatedly lost ten to twenty-five pounds. Now I go down only to 150 pounds; 145 pounds seems impossible anymore. I do a major diet about every two years. I hold the weight for a year then creep up again to one hundred seventy pounds.

Was this sudden proclivity of the body to hang onto fat a part of the biological imperative to cushion the baby in the womb? If so, it was about thirty years too late. And why, oh why, were men not piling that weight on in the same way? If it weren't bad enough that every Oreo cookie I ate flew straight onto my hips, it seems that those Oreos just gave men a flirty wave as they cruised straight through their digestive systems, never stopping to create more flab.

And then, when it comes to losing whatever extra weight men may have put on, nature really twists the knife. When I want to lose ten pounds, it means starving myself and, even worse, eating nothing that I love for at least five to six weeks. Men can lose weight simply by declaring their intention. I have timed it. At 2:05 p.m. on a Tuesday, my friend John will say, "I've got to lose some weight." At 2:10 p.m. he says, "Ha! Four pounds down!"

What's up with that? We gain it easier and we lose it harder. UNFAIR!

Unfortunately, I think I know what the deal is.

I think that men, no matter what age, are still attracted to women who can procreate, because men's hard wiring is still saying, "Make babies! Make babies!" Recently I saw an interview with Billy Joel. I'm not sure of his age, but he looks sixty-five, has difficulty with alcohol, has had several serious car accidents, and has a grown daughter. He said, "I'd like to start a family. I'd like to have a child." Say what?

So that hard wiring is there and from what I've read, it is a woman's hourglass figure that says, "She's a reproducer!" and sets men's hormones buzzing, triggering the urge to sex. A woman's shape is most "hourglass-like" when she is in her late teens and twenties when she can best produce healthy bouncing babies.

Now isn't it simple? It is evidently nature's intention to start reshaping our waists when we are past childbearing years. Nature simply does not want men to be confused and waste their seeds on the infertile. As an explanation of our transformation from hourglass to bell-shape, it makes sense. Nature doesn't want those babies to come from bodies that are not in tip-top shape for baby dropping, so it starts piling on the pounds. As a theory it even has the added advantage of explaining why otherwise loving rational men dump their faithful wives and marry the twenty-five-year-olds. The poor things think they still have to breed to populate the earth.

So, now that I understand why I pack on pounds more quickly all the time, and why my waist now stays thicker no matter how long I spend at the gym, do I feel better about it all? Can I relax and enjoy it? Can I ease into pudgy without dismay?

Hell, no. The fact is that I still want to be attractive to men, and in order to attract men, my psyche says, "Lose the weight!" So, the diets will continue, the treadmill will be run, and spandex will hold in the pounds I can't lose.

YOUR TURN
Discussion Questions:
1. Is your self-image affected by weight gain or loss? If so, how?
2. Is your daily diet geared more toward health or appearance? Would you risk your health for your appearance?
3. Would you rather be richer or thinner? Smarter or thinner? More talented or thinner? Why?

Individual Exercises:
Exercise One: *You Are Not Alone*
1. Call women friends and ask each what she considers to be her ideal weight. Then ask whether she is at her ideal weight.
2. Do not stop until you find a woman who believes she currently is at her ideal weight. If you run out of friends, start approaching strangers with the question (like in the supermarket).
3. If you reach twenty people and still haven't found a woman who feels she is at her ideal weight, you can stop.
4. What do your results indicate about women and weight? Do you dislike your own weight? What does that mean about your opinion of yourself and your worth?

Exercise Two: *Know Why You Overeat*
If you believe that you overeat, this exercise is for you.
1. Write two pages (8 x11" notebook size pages) providing endings for the following sentence: "I eat because…" Write as fast as you can. Do not judge what you are writing, just keep writing. Don't worry about repeating yourself. It doesn't matter. Fill the full two pages.
2. When you are finished, review what you have written, looking for common themes, or for repetition. Sentences near the end of the exercise generally are more truthful, more authentic, because they came at the point when your brain got tired and stopped filtering what you were writing.
3. Pick the reason that seems to be dominant in your list and commit to addressing that reason. For instance, if you wrote "I eat because I am lonely" you may want to commit to changing your reaction to loneliness to one that will benefit you. While there is no guarantee that this will change your lonely/eat

behavior, if you don't commit to change, it is guaranteed that your lonely/eat behavior will continue.

Group Exercise:
Exercise One: *Lighten Up*

1. Go around the group and ask everyone to state, in three or four sentences, her health issues.
2. Go around the group again and have each person say how her life would be different if she were completely healthy.
3. Go around a third time and have each person state one health area in which changing her habits would make a difference (*e.g.* healthy eating, not smoking).
4. Ask each person to then write down a commitment to address that area she can directly affect, and to address it by a date she chooses.
5. Have each person pick a partner. The partners tell each other their commitment and the date by which it will be accomplished. The partners agree to support each other in reaching their goals.

Exercise Two: *If All Else Fails*

For this exercise, the leader should have her bathroom scale with her and a supply of hammers for everyone in the group.

1. Form a circle.
2. Put the scale in the middle of the circle.
3. Each participant, in turn, will smash the scale with her hammer.
4. When the scale is destroyed, the exercise is complete.
5. The group can take up a collection to buy the leader a new scale should she so desire.

Assignment:

Pretend you are the fourth author of *Saving the Best for Last* and write your story about "Weighing In" in your notebook.

Memories Lost and Found

If we are an accumulation of all of our memories, then many of us are in serious trouble. Memories, like socks, often appear and disappear in random fashion. Sometimes, their appearance, like the errant sock, makes a match and we once again capture a complete memory. More often than not, the lone memory, like the lone sock whose matchless mate has long ago been discarded, simply reminds us more of what is missing than what is remembered.

Failing memories create interesting scenarios. We find ourselves adopting other people's memories, just as they adopt ours. We listen to a friend describe a funny incident and remember we were the ones who saw the incident and told our friend about it. We, in turn, entertain people at dinner parties with experiences that originally belonged to others. Our memories, like children in Socialist communes, are shared responsibilities and provide pleasure for all.

We can also benefit from the Swiss cheese-like pattern of our memories. We appear to be benevolent and forgiving, when, months or years later, we warmly greet people who have wronged us in the past. We haven't learned to forgive at all; we have simply forgotten whatever events have angered us.

We blame menopause, the hectic pace of modern life, adult ADD. Whatever works is fine. As long as we make a distinction between normal age-related memory loss and the very serious conditions of Alzheimer's and dementia, we are able to step back, take a deep breath, and keep going. We may not know which direction we are going in, but we will create movement. And movement is what it's all about.

RENEE

My ex-mother-in-law, June, was in the tiny percentage of people who contract Alzheimer's while still in their fifties. Most of us in our fifties get to know the disease through older family members' diagnoses.

Alzheimer's is unique among fatal diseases. It steals personalities before it steals lives. It is detected as much through observation as by testing. It can cause more pain to those not afflicted than to those who are.

June died just a few years ago. I had already been divorced from her son, and so I was no longer her daughter-in-law. But she will always be my mother-in-law, and I will always remember her as one of the great gifts in my life.

June came into my life when I was nineteen years old and began to date her son, Ron. Before I got to know her, I thought of her only as Ron's sole access to a car. She had a classic, a 1957 Chevy, purchased used from an ad in the paper. She laughed when teenagers would come to the door and offer to buy it from her, not fully realizing she owned a hot commodity. She tied a large plastic flower on the antenna so she could find it in parking lots. She didn't drive on highways.

When Ron and I became serious about our relationship, I began spending more time at his house. It didn't take me long to realize that June was like my own mom—loving, caring, compassionate, always putting others first. My mother, the Jewish immigrant, and June, the WASP whose family was in America before the Civil War, shared an eerily similar heart and soul.

June was my introduction to the magic of Christmas. In my observant Jewish home, Christmas was strictly off limits. Being at June's house was a blameless way for me to wallow in all of it: decorating the tree; shopping for and wrapping presents; listening to the carolers; and, staying up half the night with anticipation. Santa Claus and presents aside, June was Christmas, period.

In later years, after my mom died, June was also Thanksgiving. She spent the day in her tiny kitchen, the oven going full blast. She wore nothing but her bra on top, because the heat bothered her. As she cooked, she hummed loudly and constantly.. That was my memory of Thanksgiving: June in her bra, humming away. June's first grandchild dubbed her "La La" because of the humming. She would be forever La La to all the grandchildren.

June cared for other people's children in her home. Her decor consisted of mismatched furniture, cribs, toys stuffed into lamp tables, cartoon character bedspreads, and plastic tumblers with handles and spouts.

When my daughter Yael was born, she was diagnosed with severely high bilirubin, and my older child, Josh, was only twelve months old. My mother was already dying, and my husband had come down with pneumonia. My in-laws had come to Virginia when I went into the hospital and then stayed for a week when I came home with the baby. June drove me each day to the doctor's office. When she wasn't doing that, she was helping me take care of both babies. She never asked if she could help. She simply did whatever she saw needed doing.

A couple of years later, we were visiting my in-laws and my kids were acting like the two and three year-olds they were. June got an exasperated look on her face and said, "I don't know how you can stand that." I was so startled that I couldn't speak. The words were coming out of her mouth, but they didn't come from her. They were in direct contrast to who she was. I heard her words all day in my mind. In the evening, I told Ron, "There's something wrong with your mom."

"There's something wrong with your mom." Not memory lapse, not confusion. It was a tiny personality quirk, nothing more. A split second of impatience in a lifetime of steadiness and even temper. It took months before the memory lapses began. It took even more time before anyone else noticed what I knew in my gut. All I was aware of was that she was leaving.

Ron and I bought a rental property at the beach, and my father-in-law decided he and June would move there. June always loved the beach and life would be simpler for her there. She was terrified of leaving, but she finally agreed. Their house was sold, and the packing was completed. On the day the movers came, she couldn't be found. She was behind the house, intending to re-brick the driveway.

The ensuing years were filled with increasingly frequent memory lapses, confusion, inappropriate behavior, and arguments over the smallest of incidents. My father-in-law held her hand when they walked, he cooked and cleaned, he washed and combed her hair, and he drove her everywhere. When he could no longer care for her himself, he put her into a nursing home.

Over time, June became more and more sluggish, distant, and docile. Her vocabulary shrank daily, and her ability to recognize people became unpredictable. Stuffed animals took the place of the homeless creatures she used to shelter, and cheery greeting cards throughout the room spouted tender thoughts she was no longer able to verbalize. A small rag doll in her arms took the place of the children she raised, the children she cared for, and the grandchildren she adored.

When Ron and I split up, I got into my car and drove several hours to the nursing home. I sat on a chair next to her bed, and I choked my way through the details of the break up of our marriage. I told her all my shameful secrets, and I asked her to forgive me. I told her that I loved her and that I needed her to love me. There was no response from her, no indication that she either recognized me or heard what I was saying. I didn't care. I spoke to the person she had been, to the person I loved.

That was the last time I saw June.

During June's funeral service, a sudden sense of peace replaced my grief. I was aware of June's presence, and I was aware of an enormous feeling of comfort and well being. I had been struggling with the idea of another woman living in my life: being Ron's wife; sleeping in my house; sitting on my furniture; and, entertaining by my pool. Although I didn't want that life again, I didn't know how my life could be otherwise. That day, when I sensed June's presence, I felt, for the first time, strong enough and competent enough to create whatever life I desired in the years to come. Beyond her untimely death, she continued to be a gift in my life.

JOYCE

Recently when traveling with a friend, I told him that I had finished a lengthy report the night before. He asked me the name of the report. I couldn't think of it. He asked me the subject of the report. I couldn't remember that, either. Four days later, while touring a museum, I remembered the name of the report. I wanted to send up a flare.

I could laugh about my memory lapses, and I do laugh sometimes, but mostly I find them scary. Today I went to get my recipe book from the bookcase. When I got to the bookcase, I straightened up the papers that needed tidying. When I went back into the kitchen, I remembered that I needed to get the cookbook from the bookcase. Returning a second time to the bookcase, I noticed something else that immediately diverted me from my purpose. Back in the kitchen, I remembered the cookbook I needed. Three trips to the bookcase and thirty minutes later, I finally had the recipe in hand.

For most of my life, I prided myself on my ability to remember faces and names. As a teacher with two hundred new students each fall, I amazed my students with my skill at memorizing all their names by the second day of classes. For years after their graduation, at reunions and other events, I was still able to recall their names. As Director of Volunteer Services, I knew the names of nearly seven hundred volunteers.

Now I am often befuddled and embarrassed when unable to remember a person's name, especially in situations requiring personal introductions. I am dumbfounded that I cannot remember something I read or saw an hour earlier.

List making has always been my thing, too. I used to keep lists of tasks to be done and what to buy at the grocery store. Now I write down when to take medications, when to submit an invoice, and what's on the menu for company (the menu I'm cooking). I can make plans for two simultaneous events without ever realizing I've done so until it's almost the time when I must be in two places at the same time. Even a Palm Pilot does not resolve this issue because I forget to consult the calendar on it.

While many of these memory lapses are annoying, inconvenient, embarrassing, and sometimes laughable, I am most self-conscious about my memory (or lack of one) at work. I am chagrined every time I cannot remember a fact, date, name, or task. I find nothing funny about this.

Fear is what I experience: fear that my failure to recall a fact or name draws attention to my age. At such times, I believe that every person I work with is as keenly aware of my memory breakdown as I am. I fear that they think I am too old, incompetent, not up to the challenge.

When my fear surfaces, I must remind myself that in the context of my work, the lapses are momentary blips on the screen. I acknowledge that my capricious memory has no impact on the quality of what I produce, and the trade-off for a not-so-great memory is that I bring the wisdom, experience, and skills of a lifetime to my work.

No one questions the caliber of my work. I seem to be the only one second-guessing myself. I am often asked to do things that no one else on the staff does as well as I do. A global organization selected me to travel alone to Africa for two months to collect stories and data to prepare a critical health document. That project took me to rural areas of three countries and comprised many hours of interviewing and writing. Because of the voluminous data I was required to collect, I bolstered my memory with a tape recorder and copious notes.

That's all I can do. I adapt. I do the best I can with what I have. In this country's culture of youth, stigma and discrimination are often associated with aging. Look at the term "senior moment." You do not hear comparable terms such as "youth moment" or "middle-age moment" when younger people are forgetful. "Senior moment" connotes powerlessness: seniors are hopeless victims to their failing memories. The term draws attention, tying memory lapse to age. It does not serve us. I do not use the term myself, even jokingly, as it is not empowering.

I continue to nurture my mind. My personal prescription for a healthy mind is to challenge it with new ideas and concepts, to learn new things. One of the main reasons I love my work is that I am always learning something new, and my work requires me to use my mind. I also keep my mind lively by writing, reading, participating in workshops, taking courses, and traveling.

Remembering to laugh when my memory trips me up, instead of freaking out, helps too.

JEAN

> The name of the author is the first to go followed obediently by the title, the plot, the heartbreaking conclusion, the entire novel which suddenly becomes one you have never read, never even heard of, as if,

one by one, the memories you used to harbor decided
to retire to the southern hemisphere of the brain, to a
little fishing village where there are no phones.

—From "Forgetfulness" by Billy Collins

I used to think this poem was cute. I thought it was a little clever,
a little amusing and maybe even a little light-hearted. Perhaps that is
because when I first read it I had just begun having trouble remembering
the authors of novels. Hah. I should have known to pay attention to
the rest of that stanza! I took the poem as poetic overstatement when,
in fact, it only describes the very tip of the memory-loss iceberg.

The poem is funny? Not when this afternoon I dropped the plastic
bag with a cut up lemon inside into a drawer, only to be discovered as
I was putting the box of sandwich bags into the refrigerator. Not funny
when I indulge (frequently) in my recent favorite pastime: parallel
planning. Parallel planning is when you happily plan two different
activities to fill the same time and space such as: Tuesday evening at
7:00 p.m., play bridge with the ladies; Tuesday evening at 7:00 p.m.,
go to the Recreation Center board meeting. The amazing thing is I
can be talking about each event and planning each for a considerable
period of time without realizing that I have double-scheduled. In other
words, this isn't like I accepted one invitation three weeks ago and
forgot about it. I can accept an invitation on Sunday at 2:00 p.m. for
Tuesday at 7:00 p.m., and then accept another invitation Sunday at
4:30 p.m. for the very same Tuesday at 7:00 p.m. I simply have no
memory of making the first appointment.

Now that is scary. That is no longer cute.

I once had a prodigious memory. I could review investigative
files piled three feet high on my desk, remember all the data therein,
and find a link between one sentence in volume one and a piece of
information in volume three. I would know exactly where in volumes
one and three that one sentence could be found and whose testimony
and at what part of the testimony it was located. I would know it right
after I reviewed the files, and I would know it three months or even a
year later. Within my office I was known for the ability to recall key
facts from voluminous data.

I also could remember everything I had ever said to another person on any topic. In fact, not only could I remember what I told him or her, I could tell you when the conversation was held, and what each of us was wearing at the time.

Lo, how the mighty have lost their memories. Last week, when I was staying with a friend in New York, I brushed my teeth and walked out of her bathroom. Fine, except I left the water running in the sink. Even worse, my friend, not I, discovered it.

When this memory loss stuff started happening to me, a co-worker offered this, "Well, you just have so much in your brain that it is overloaded and simply cannot contain all you have to remember." Baloney. And so what if my brain is overloaded? What am I supposed to do? Take some information out of my brain every day and put it in a filing cabinet? "Let's see, I don't foresee any need for the German language today, let's just file it under World War II."

Another friend offered, "Oh that always happens to me too. I just can't remember people's names anymore." Baloney. People's names have been gone for years. Now I am re-naming other things. The other day I called the Home Depot "Top Job." I don't know why. It is the name that came when I was trying to say I was headed out to buy some paint.

The most creative comment came from a friend who is into Eastern thought, "I think your mind is just simplifying your life for you." Baloney. I know that people say things just to smooth over a difficult social situation, but for some of us, it just doesn't work.

For the last ten years of her life, my grandmother had Alzheimer's. The signal to the family that Gram no longer could live alone was when she repeatedly forgot to turn the flame off under the tea kettle. My mother took care of her until the stress was too great, and Gram went into a nursing home. She died in 1990. Ten years later, in 2000, my mother was diagnosed with Alzheimer's.

Alzheimer's is a horrible disease that left my grandmother and mother alive in body only. They lived their last years knowing almost no one, and tortured with fear and terror. When you have Alzheimer's in the family, it is difficult to separate what is "natural" memory loss from what might be a precursor to Alzheimer's or some other form of dementia. By nature, I am not a worrier. If something is not directly in my control, I tend not to spend much time stressing over it. With memory loss, however, and the shadow of Alzheimer's, I do find myself bringing up th e subject of memory loss with friends so that I might covertly compare how they are doing versus my experience of myself.

So although I laugh along with others when I do things like make a list to take to the store as a memory aid, forget to take the list with me, and forget why I went to the store at all, beneath my laughter is fear and worry.

I read somewhere that one defense against Alzheimer's is dancing. Ah! What great news. There may be my defense; there may be my salvation. I dance at least once a week. I have a dance partner who hero-worships Fred Astaire and John Travolta. We swoop, we glide, we dip, we wiggle, we giggle.

If indeed, dance is my rescue vehicle, it truly is a miracle. First, because I already am dancing; and second, it will be the first time ever that something I love is also good for me. Alcohol, cigarettes, food, and '70s drugs all turned out to be false friends. But dancing! What a joy that what I love could also save my memory and my sanity!

YOUR TURN
Discussion Questions:
1. Have you experienced a change in your ability to remember? Describe the change. Why do you think this is happening? Is it the natural result of aging or due to external factors?
2. If you are still employed, are memory concerns greater? How do you cope? What are your fears concerning memory?
3. Have you had experience with Alzheimer's or dementia in your family or with friends? Have you educated yourself about Alzheimer's or dementia?
4. If there were a test to determine whether you have Alzheimer's disease, would you take it? Why or why not?

Individual Exercise: *Learn to Cope*
1. Interview six women: one in her thirties, one in her forties, one in her fifties, one in her sixties, one in her seventies, and one in her eighties. Ask each whether she considers herself to have a good memory, a fair memory, or poor memory.
2. Ask each to tell you how she has coped with memory issues.
3. When you are finished, compile their suggestions into one document. Put the document away, and try to find it in one year. No, but really, when you are finished, keep the document as a resource when you need it.

Group Exercise: *Why We Remember, Why We Forget*
1. Divide the group into pairs. Each pair will pick a Partner A and a Partner B.
2. Partner A will ask Partner B the following questions.
   - What is your earliest memory?
   - Where were you?
   - What were you wearing?
   - Who else was there?
   - Then ask, what did you have for lunch yesterday? The day before?
3. Reverse roles with Partner B asking the same questions of Partner A. Then discuss the following.
   - What makes some memories stay and others leave?
   - Do you think that memory loss is natural, or can it be avoided?

• Do you think memory loss reflects on you in some way?

Assignment:

Pretend you are the fourth author of *Saving the Best for Last* and write your story about "Memories Lost and Found" in your notebook.

Money Honey

Money means more than dollars. It's tied to our sense of success, to security, to power, to independence. It can be what allows us, or stops, us from fulfilling our dreams. And, for most women, it's something we don't give much thought to until we are confronted with a major life change.

For those of us who experience divorce, it may be the first time in our lives that we have to think about our own financial security. The years following midlife present additional challenges. Retirement looms, and with it, the awareness that, the desire for freedom aside, we may be less than comfortable about giving up a steady income. Topics such as long-term care and Medicare necessitate far more brainpower than we ever needed in order to earn our advanced degrees. And somehow, our children assuring us that they will always care for us financially isn't enough to have us liquidate our bank accounts and take a round-the-world tour.

Some of us, even those who have been financially successful in life, walk around convinced that we will end up bag ladies in our final years. We may feel this way in spite of what our bank statement shows. We are afraid to spend money on anything other than a shopping cart. Others of us may continue to spend money as though it will always be there, and the farthest we get toward retirement planning is to buy an occasional lottery ticket.

Whatever our conversation about money, we own it to the same degree we get to own our wardrobes. Whether we are married or not, whether we are working or not, whether we are healthy or not, we get to take ownership of our financial well-being. Most importantly, we get to use it to save not just for some point in the distant future but to create what we want for our lives right now. Whatever we create right now *will* determine our future.

RENEE

Being the only child of my parents and the only grandchild of my grandparents, I grew up with an abundance of virtually everything that mattered: love, care, and attention. I grew up secure, knowing no one was smarter, or more beautiful, or more talented than I was. My family gave me what they could emotionally, as they did not have access to unlimited financial resources. Money was always in short supply.

My father, an Eastern European Jewish immigrant, grew up in extreme poverty. From age thirteen, he had to work full-time. Making money beyond the bare minimum necessary to buy food and keep a roof over our heads would have meant taking risks. My father was happy to have left Europe with his life. That, for him, was enough risk for a lifetime.

Before age ten, I was pretty much oblivious to my family's lack of money. I tried to ignore the strange person who was renting one of our bedrooms while he attended the optometry college at the corner. I thought everyone had a boarder in their house. I also thought all furniture came from family members who were tired of it, and the only new items anyone could get were those that could be obtained from supermarket stamp redemption centers.

From age ten on, I suffered. In late elementary school, the crinoline craze swept through my school with the intensity of Dorothy's tornado. At parties, girls pranced around with their skirts fluffed out at ninety-degree angles to their bodies. A favorite activity was pulling up one's skirt and counting the layers underneath. My skirt lay flat against my legs, a sad flag on a windless day.

My family didn't own a car. I had heard rumors about "Sunday drives." When my family wanted to get from Point A to Point B, we had one of three options: subway, bus, or feet. Many times, it was a combination of all three forms of transportation that took us anywhere. The thought of simply deciding to travel somewhere that didn't involve a job or a doctor at the other end was a total mystery to me.

When my school announced it was having a summer camp one year, I was thrilled. I was familiar with this thing called "camp" in books I had read. My head swirled with visions of a swimming pool (forget the fact that I had never been in a pool and had not the vaguest idea how to swim) and green grass and trees. I planned to ride horses, toast marshmallows at campfires, and go on nature walks (another mystery activity).

The reality was that I got to walk each day to the elementary school where I would sit at a picnic table on the concrete playground making "crafts." At the end of the summer, I had third-degree burns on my face and a lifetime supply of plastic lanyards and multi-colored, looped potholders. To this day, the sight of a potholder makes me woozy.

Eventually, I got my wish. At age fourteen, I was fortunate enough to be accepted to a camp for "underprivileged Jewish children." (Yes, they *do* exist.) I had a great experience, and, with the exception of horseback riding, I got to experience for the first time swimming in a pool, sleeping in a cabin, and sitting around a campfire. At the end-of-camp closing assembly, members of the Board of Directors of the foundation that ran the camp explained to us in great detail how their generosity was all that stood between us and a lifetime of crime and drug abuse. I applauded wildly, simply happy to have avoided another summer of sunstroke and potholders.

My parents and I didn't eat in restaurants, go to the movies, or take family vacations. Anywhere. We did go to Atlantic City on day trips, when a charitable family member would drive us there. We arrived wearing our bathing suits and took a change of clothes with us. We changed out of our sandy bathing suits in the public bathroom on the boardwalk. I crawled under the stall door and opened it for my mother, so she could avoid the nickel it took to open the door. While I was more than happy to help my mom, I am now more familiar than I'd like to be with toilet stall floors.

When I was fifteen, I got my first real summer job and so, for the first time, entered the giddy world of disposable income. From that moment on, I bought all of my own clothes, albeit clothes that were purchased from discount stores. I never looked back. I worked through summers in high school and sometimes on weekends. I delayed my entry into college so I could work full-time to save money for tuition.

I took any job that would have me. Name a job. If it didn't involve a college degree, or the ability to climb scaffolding, or save your life in a swimming pool, I had it. I can fit you for a bra, sell you Tupperware, watch your children, serve your family dinner by balancing all the plates on my arms, or run errands involving purchasing your cigars. I can file, type, collate, deliver, stamp, bill, research, edit, and review. I can even pose for you in your art studio, but that's another story entirely.

I learned that the world didn't automatically owe me anything. And because nothing was handed to me, I got to put a lot of thought into what I did want. Everything was of greater value when I earned it myself. There was incomparable joy in the earning and the anticipation. I came to savor the planning more than the purchase. Delayed gratification became my middle name. And, throughout the early years of my marriage, it allowed me to stay focused while saving for a car, a house, furniture, vacations, everything. After the children were born, it allowed me to remain cheerful without having the ability to take showers.

Although initially trained as a teacher (stable, predictable, safe), I had moved on to selling real estate and was loving it. My income fluctuated (not stable, predictable or safe), but my husband's income was good and so my income was a bonus. The end of my marriage, however, coincided with a serious dip in the real estate market. I was in my late forties and had three children. To top it off, my guilt about my behavior during the last year of my marriage prompted me to leave without a monetary settlement.

Was I scared? You bet. During that first year of my separation, I kept the thermostat low in the winter and didn't use air conditioning in the summer. I took no vacations, rarely ate out, and was grateful that public restrooms no longer necessitated nickels for entry.

Even more difficult than my poor finances was the realization that I had allowed my husband to be in control of what was always in my control: my financial well-being. He made choices about our investments, did our taxes, and kept track of our net worth. I allowed him to make decisions about our financial life, just as I allowed him to make decisions about our marriage.

The first few years were tough, and I'm not talking about the huge drop in my net worth and disposable income. I had to reclaim ownership of my own financial well-being. I had to painstakingly work my way back to the eighteen-year-old who decided on her own what she would do with her first real paycheck. I had to be responsible for my thousands of dollars with the same degree of maturity that she had with her hundreds. I made some big mistakes along the way, and I survived.

My relationship with money is not attached to personal emotion, because I established a relationship with my life when I had *no* money. The dream came first, the money later. I do not chase the money; I chase the dream. Like intelligence, creativity, and the capacity to love and be loved, money is simply one more tool I can access to create my life.

JOYCE

"Money doesn't grow on trees" was a comment I often heard when I was young. It was one of my earliest lessons about money. My siblings and I knew not to ask my parents to buy us anything. I was to earn money, not ask for it.

Money was always in short supply in our household because my father was the sole breadwinner, and he was often unemployed or underemployed. He also gambled on horses. My mother didn't work outside the home because she had seven children and my grandfather to care for.

When my sisters and I were old enough, we earned money when elderly neighbors hired us to scrub floors and the white marble steps of our Baltimore row houses. My brothers hauled groceries at the A&P and picked up discarded glass soda bottles around the neighborhood to redeem for cash. But we usually gave our money to my mother who used it for necessities. Occasionally, we were allowed to keep our earnings but only to purchase something we really needed, such as a notebook for school.

Food on the table was often a one-dish meal, and my parents went without at times. Our clothes were always hand-me-downs from neighbors or relatives. I hated holidays because they brought into focus how poor we were. I would sometimes cry myself to sleep in anticipation of my brothers' and sisters' disappointment on Christmas mornings when there would be little or nothing under the tree for them. Other times, donations of food and used toys from the Salvation Army appeared at our door at the last minute on Christmas Eve. I felt sad and ashamed about how we lived but helpless to change the situation.

When my father went to the penitentiary, my mother's only means of supporting the seven of us was to go on welfare. Our family car was repossessed, we were not allowed a telephone, and we older kids took turns walking to the Welfare Department several miles away to get food handouts. I tried to hide the facts of our lives from everyone I knew, and I avoided bringing friends to my house because I didn't want them to see how we lived. I would get sick to my stomach at the thought of anyone coming into my house. I hated the way we lived. I was angry, but I had no control and felt powerless to change it.

I longed to be like other kids. I wanted a "normal" family like the one portrayed in "Father Knows Best" on television or like the families I saw in my neighborhood. "Normal" meant having a kind father who provided for the family's needs, having a home where one could invite friends, and having enough income to provide more than bare necessities. I never thought we were normal, and it was yet one more secret for me to hide.

I tried to be like my peers. In high school I wanted to work so that I could buy clothes and pay for my school ring and prom gown. My mother understood, but my new-found income from working at Kresge's dime store at age seventeen meant I was taken off the welfare roll, and my mother got even less money each month. I did not contribute to our household but used my earnings for my own needs. My mother still fed me and kept a roof over my head, but after I left home at eighteen and until now, I have supported myself.

Underneath my embarrassment of poverty and guilt for turning in my father to the police, I felt like I was nothing. These thoughts and emotions provided the seed for my drive to "better" myself. I became a woman on a mission to prove I was above my circumstances. Bettering myself meant I had to make my own money and do something respectable to get out of South Baltimore—thus my plan to go to college and become a teacher. The education and career would take me out of the ghetto; I would be able to improve my life and with it, gain the esteem I craved. I would be respected and valued.

But I also knew that if I wanted to go to college, I had to find my own way, so I studied and worked to earn a scholarship. With scholarships, National Defense Loans, and working part-time, I was able to put myself through college and get a teaching degree. That degree was my ticket out of poverty. My mother was pleased because I would always have something to fall back on; but, to me, it was never a fallback career. It was all I ever wanted.

When I married, I worked several jobs a year so that my husband could have the opportunity to "better" himself. I don't know how we survived, but life was much easier in the early 1960s when we could buy food on far less money than now. Though we had little disposable income, I experienced pride that I had finished college and had launched my career. Despite the low pay for Baltimore City teachers, I never again felt poor or ashamed. I had become the person I aspired to be. I had proven that I was better than the circumstances under which I was raised.

My esteem grew when my husband and I opened a plant store in the 1970s with very little capital and created a successful, well-respected business. It involved a risk—borrowing several thousand dollars with no business experience—but it was a calculated risk. If the business wasn't successful, my husband and I could afford to repay the money over time. However, sales thrived, and we quickly repaid the loan. All went well until he and I separated, and our personal problems interfered with the business so much that we had to close the store. I went back to teaching to support myself as we moved toward divorce.

After the divorce, I found a new business partner, and we bought out my ex-husband's half of the property where the plant store had been. In short order, we bought three other investment properties with no cash. Risk-taking was exciting, and I told myself that I had lived with a low income before, so if my partner and I couldn't handle the finances and lost our properties, so be it. I could pick myself up and start anew; at least that's what I told myself. Most of this new attitude had to do with my partner's relationship with risk and finance. Because she was unattached to the results of our investing, I too experienced more freedom to take risks. Lucky for us, it all worked out, and we were successful at selling the properties later at a considerable profit.

Later during my fifties, she and I started a consulting business where we looked forward to educating companies on how to deal with AIDS in the workplace. We failed. My partner had other sources of income, but I used up all my savings and relied on my credit cards to pay my mortgage and other living expenses.

When we closed the doors to our company I had a great deal of personal debt, and we also had a business line of credit to pay off. The concept of financial failure had always been somewhat scary to me and was a looming boogey man, even during times of success. My pride at being self-sufficient was at stake right then, right there.

Once I was face-to-face with the reality of financial and business failure, I discovered I had it within myself to respond responsibly. I took a deep breath and took it on. I did not spiral back to shame or embarrassment because I developed a plan and I worked it out, repaying all my debts while at the same time creating a new, more lucrative career for myself in international AIDS work. From that point on, I was okay.

With my international consulting business flourishing, I had more disposable income than I'd ever had in my life. I felt rich and I could play. I could contribute money to my favorite charities. I traveled more, bought whatever I wanted, and began gambling simply because I could.

Residual fears and my memory of poverty receded into the background. I loved playing the slots, and they became a recreation, an escape from my everyday life, people, and work. I could zone out. I could be alone and not have to think about anything except the machine in front of me. It felt good not to be so super responsible. I have read that female gamblers gamble for time away from their problems but create financial problems because of it. That description certainly fit me. Becoming unconscious was not new but gambling was a new way to reach a familiar feeling.

It was thrilling and fun to visit casinos until I realized how much money and time I squandered and how reckless I was with my money. Eventually, the amount of money I spent gambling made my life just as difficult as it had been when I made less money and had to scrimp to make ends meet. I finally admitted I had a problem and took steps to bring my addiction under control.

Gamblers Anonymous and therapy helped, but I noticed how I don't like to admit I have a problem. In my way of thinking, it implies I am not totally self-sufficient. I can't go it alone. Asking for help is still hard, but I know I must be responsible.

Until I was in my mid-fifties I never thought about old age or planned for my future. I knew I would have some retirement income from teaching (how little I never knew), but I never saved much money because I earned so little as a teacher. And like many people, when I was younger I could not see myself reaching the age I am now or imagine what it would be like. I had always managed to scrape by and create the money I needed when I needed it, so I wasn't very concerned about the future. I assumed I would deal with it when the time came.

That time was now. I hired a financial planner. With discipline and planning, I have been saving money and taking the steps I need to give myself financial security. I wrote a will, created some investments, bought a long-term disability plan, and set up a budget for the first time.

My relationship with money has evolved from one of embarrassment and avoidance in my youth to self-sufficiency and responsibility. One of the joys of aging is that it brings some wisdom and, thus, money and work no longer have total power to determine my worth as a human being. Money has the value and meaning I place on it. And even though I have enough, residual fear still can rear its head. The fear lingers but is not controlling.

JEAN

I grew up the child of survivors of the Great Depression of the 1930s. My parents married in 1938, and they frequently talked about how Dad made $8.00 a week at the fountain pen factory. This promising career was cut off by the invention of the ballpoint pen. What seemed to be a tragedy turned out to be an opportunity: the fountain pen factory owner, being depressed both emotionally and financially, gave Dad the remaining stock of fountain pens. Dad became a salesman, taking the stock around to offices and businesses that had not yet discovered the new-fangled ballpoint pen.

Lest anyone think that this made my father a real go-getter, let me explain. My mother was the go-getter, my father carried out her directives. My father epitomized the anti-ambition movement that flowered for a golden moment decades later in the hippie era. If there were a newspaper, he would read it. If there were a stream, he would fish it. If there were a promotion, he would turn it down.

When my father, in wartime (and when the pens ran out) went to work in an airplane factory, he was quickly offered a promotion to foreman. He rejected it just as quickly. Years later, he made the transition from blue to white collar by becoming an insurance salesman. Nothing else changed. He was offered a management position, and he rejected it. My mother, who secretly wanted to run the world, was mightily frustrated by this gentle man who just wanted to live honorably and with a small footprint.

In my family, the accumulation of money was never presented as a goal in itself. It was not lusted after. It was saved, guarded, and used wisely. I knew we weren't rich because there were rich kids in school, and I saw the difference. I remember noticing that when my parents' friends talked about rich people, there was an edge to their voices. It was clear that "their" lives were not the same as "our" lives, and there seemed to be a shared belief that we were somehow more morally sound than they were. It is the view of the have-nots toward the haves.

I also knew there were kids in my class who were really poor. Their clothes were ill fitting, and they came to school without lunch. They seemed to have nothing we had, no new bikes or clothes, or anything. My parents said they were on welfare. Just as excess money bespoke moral failings of some sort, so did too little money. While we were a bit vague about the exact nature of the moral failings of the rich, we were quite clear about the other end of the spectrum. If you had no money, it was because you either were too lazy to earn it or too undisciplined to safeguard it.

In my childhood, money was to be used only for necessities and for as few necessities as possible. That's why I never owned more than three bras at a time. I had five pairs of underpants, but that was only because my aunt worked sewing crotches in an underpants factory. She would bring us "seconds" that otherwise would have been thrown away.

None of my friends had more than three bras at a time, three sturdy white cotton bras. I absolutely have marked in my memory the day I bought a new bra even though I already owned the limit of three. I was thirty-five years old. And by the time I realized I really could buy something other than sturdy white cotton bras, I was over forty and in need of under wire support.

My parents gave regularly to the church. I cannot remember them giving to any other charity, although it is possible that they did. I think that any other cause would have to meet a pretty tough criterion. The object would have to be worthy—meaning "not their own fault." Childhood disease would be worthy; feeding the homeless would not. Whatever the cause, and it may have been a basic frugality born of the Depression, my parents were not generous with their money.

It is amazing that I absorbed all of these things as a child because no one ever talked about money in my family—especially about how much or how little money one had. I once told a girlfriend, within my mother's earshot, that my parents couldn't afford braces for me. My mother yanked me out of the room and made it oh-so-clear that one did *not* share such information outside the family. That implanted in my mind the notion that one's financial situation was something never to be discussed.

The strongest lesson I learned in my childhood was that it is critically important to be financially secure and to prepare for the future. Be thrifty. Work hard. The purpose of being thrifty and working hard was to achieve financial security. It was, seemingly, a perfect formula.

When I was in my late thirties, everything I ever thought I knew about money was blown to hell. At age thirty-seven, I was in law school, a single mother with two children, and three jobs. I was near exhaustion, but I was being thrifty and working hard. Not only was I paying my own way through law school (while the law school had scholarships for veterans, they wouldn't buy my theory that I was a marriage veteran), I was taking care of my kids, going to class, and studying. I was very proud that I had managed, out of my minimum wage jobs, to put $1,500 into a savings account. "The children's' college fund" I called it.

At the beginning of my third year of law school, I was struck down by a mystery disease. I was hospitalized for about three weeks, during which the condition was diagnosed variously as pneumonia, Legionnaire's Disease, and, finally, a pulmonary thrombosis, a blood clot in my lungs. The cause of the clot was vague but thought to be a combination of smoking, a history of taking birth control pills, and my age. I escaped with my life but with my belief in financial security out the window.

All of my jobs were hourly jobs. During those three weeks, since I didn't work, I didn't get paid. Within one month, my savings were gone, I had no money to feed the children or pay the bills, and I was $10,000 in debt to the doctors and the hospital. I had been thrifty and worked hard. I had done everything "right," yet here I was, financially shattered.

All of my reactions to the discovery that security did not exist were negative. For the next five years, I couldn't pay my bills in any normal manner. Even when the money to pay them was in my checking account, I couldn't make myself spend it because then it would be gone, and "something" might happen wherein I would need it! As a result, although I now was out of law school and making a decent living working for the government, my lights and my telephone service were being turned off regularly. Creditors were dunning me constantly. I saved no money because I was always paying late fines and fees. It eventually got so bad that I stopped opening my mail because I no longer wanted to look at the bills. I was filled with shame that I wasn't being responsible and with fear that others would know about it.

An understanding, loving friend saved me. I never would have revealed my shame to anyone, but somehow my friend Deborah got my secret from me. She then made the best offer ever. She would take my basketful of unopened mail, sort through it all, and contact all my creditors to set up payment schedules. The offer went further. Deborah knew I was in the grip of a paralysis that had not yet been healed, so she offered to be the person who actually paid my bills, from my checking account, for whatever period I needed her to do that.

Deborah paid my bills for one year. Then I tried for a month or two to pay the bills myself. At bill pay time I would begin to sweat and shake. My stomach knotted and spasmed. Although I paid the bills those months, the physical and emotional toll was ridiculous. So, not having the money to hire a shrink to sort through this mental/emotional block, I instead hired my older daughter, then about age fifteen, to take over Deborah's job and pay the bills. That continued for a couple of years.

When my daughter went off to college, I again needed to pay my own bills. The cost to do so was still there, although not as severe. I would avoid, delay, and dread the first of the month. I would set aside a whole evening as though I were planning the yearly audit of a major corporation instead of just paying my eight or ten bills. I surrounded the event with a lot of ritual—the "pay it all" bills in this pile, the "pay part of it" in this pile. Before I wrote a single check, I figured and refigured how various formulas of payments would affect the bottom line of money left in the checking account so I'd know how much money was left for emergencies. What if I paid all bills in full? What if I paid only half of the Sears bill this month and the entire electric bill? I moved the paper bills from pile to pile as I figured. I actually measured the height of each pile to see if that was a good factor to use to decide what to pay.

It wasn't until I was over fifty that I was able to entertain the idea that maybe the impossibility of being "secure" wasn't a bad thing. And just maybe it wasn't my personal tragedy or failing that there was no security but simply *life*. The victory of that new understanding was that it became easier to pay my bills. Two other factors helped ease my bill-paying trauma. First, I tried paying bills as they came in. The payoff for that was that I avoided the monthly ritual entirely. That was worth risking not having "enough" money at the end of the month. Secondly, I switched to electronic bill paying. This allowed me to avoid my love affair with the paper involved in bill paying. No piles to measure anymore.

I see now that my belief that we must create financial security through hard work and thrift is a wonderful example of a good principle that has outlived its usefulness and become a liability. I can see how, in the Depression, the lack of money—the poverty—created the sanctity of the principle of security. It served my parents well. The problem is that they passed that on to me as an unquestioned rule. The disaster that befell me did so with no regard for the fact that I had done everything "right." I could see that although we can strive for it, security can always disappear, and disappear suddenly. I realized that while I will always work toward it, I will never ever again believe there are any guarantees of security.

Further, I began to see the liability of having security as one's primary principle. The emphasis on it can be the death of dreams. I stayed in government work with one agency for twenty-one years because I was afraid to let go of the income and future pension. I rejected opportunities to leap into something great because I was afraid to let go of the security I had. It wasn't until I was fifty-nine years old that I said "enough" and leaped into the future I wanted. I am living the life I want to live, and, even better, the money I make is enough so that I didn't abandon security altogether.

I am grateful to my parents for what they taught me but have chosen some new principles for my life. Money is less important than living fully and passionately. Money is neither good nor evil, thus having it or not having it has no intrinsic value. Talking about money can open whole new areas of connection with my family and friends, removing its once taboo status. Sharing money with others is an expression of gratitude and, as such, is important to me.

Living my passion is what matters. If there is a rainy day, I will get an umbrella.

YOUR TURN
Discussion Questions:
1. What beliefs about money did you learn as a child? Do you still have those beliefs? Do they work for you?
2. What are your patterns of spending and saving money? Do they reflect your vision for your life?
3. If you have a partner, how are your beliefs about money influenced by your partner's beliefs?
4. Are you frequently in debt or do you worry that you may have an addiction that could threaten your financial security? Why? Have you dealt with it? If so, how? If not, why not?
5. Is financial security important to you? What does financial security look like to you? Do you feel financially secure? Will you ever feel financially secure? Why or why not?

Individual Exercise: *Follow the Money*
1. For one month, keep track in your notebook of every penny you spend. Include large monthly expenses like mortgage or utilities, and don't forget small expenditures like your skim latte.
2. At the end of the month, set aside at least an hour to review where your money went. Do your expenditures reflect your vision for your life? Are you spending responsibly? Would any of your expenditures embarrass you if others knew about them? Why?
3. If you wish, construct a budget that will allow you to live within your means.

Group Exercise: *Priorities*
The purpose of this exercise is to look at the priorities in your life and their relationship to one another.
1. Give a copy of the following list to each participant
   * Financial Security
   * Love
   * Wisdom
   * Faith/Spirituality
   * Travel
   * Career
   * Fame

- Sex
- Family
- Friendship

2. Each participant will rank the ten items in order of importance to her life, from most to least important.

3. Discuss the top three items and the bottom three items on each person's list. Are they very different from each other? Do we all desire pretty much the same thing or not? Explore why and how people chose their top three items.

4. Where did financial security rank in comparison with other priorities? Are you comfortable with this?

Assignment:

Pretend you are the fourth author of *Saving the Best for Last* and write your story about "Money."

The Realities of Breast Cancer

Our breasts. As young girls, we hunger for them. As young women, we bear them proudly. As maturing women, we lure both babies and men to us by their presence. We can nourish our young or make men salivate, all by using them. Whether we flaunt them, enhance them, make them bigger or smaller, they are, to a great extent, the visible manifestation of who and what we are as women. For this reason, breast cancer attacks us on a dual level. It not only threatens our lives, it threatens our identities.

We call this chapter the *realities* of breast cancer because, often, the public face of breast cancer is different from the private. There are as many stories about the experience of breast cancer as there are women who have fought the disease and those who have loved these women. It would be impossible to cover the gamut of emotions and experiences.

We three, through some mysterious quirk of fate, have lived through what might be several of the most common experiences of breast cancer. Joyce is a survivor and lost her mother to breast cancer. Jean lost her sister to breast cancer. Her daughter and her other sister are survivors. Renee lost one of her best friends. And all of this occurred when we were close to or over age fifty. Until our late forties, the effect of breast cancer was, for us, something that happened to *other* people. By midlife, it was something that happened to *us*.

We three found our own ways to cope and to grieve. But something more important happened. From our grief, we made choices for our lives, choices that might not have been made otherwise. And it is these choices that impact our lives to this day.

RENEE

I participated in the first annual Avon Breast Cancer Walk in Washington, D.C., sixty miles from Frederick, Maryland, to the grounds of the Washington Monument. This story is not about blisters or sleeping in a tent. Neither is it about unrelenting ninety degree heat or being awakened during the night by other walkers slamming Porta-potty doors. It is not about hills that never ran out or toilet paper that did. It is not even about powdered eggs, although goodness knows, someone somewhere should take on the banning of powdered egg production as a personal crusade.

It is, instead, about three women. It is about my friend Miki and all the Mikis in our lives who lived out loud while death quietly waited. It is about my friend Joyce and all the Joyces in our lives who fought for life every day, heroically, and without self-pity, and whose ultimate reward was to live to fight another day. It is about my daughter, Yael, who declared the impossible and then made it happen. It is about whatever that spirit is that creates the extraordinary out of the ordinary. I chose to have that for my life, as well, and so I chose the impossible.

My friend Miki chose to turn a death sentence into an unshakeable commitment to her daughter. On an ordinary day, over chicken Caesar salads, we talked. She was seated across from me, wearing a bandana to cover her hairless scalp, the ravages of chemotherapy so obvious on her face.

"Each day I survive, my daughter is one day older," she said to me. The statement was so utterly simple, the words spoken by the same statuesque woman who used to wear bikinis, turn men's heads, and make me laugh at the world in a way no one has ever done since. In that moment in the restaurant, she had never been so beautiful.

Joyce survives, has in fact survived, far more than breast cancer in her life. When I first met her, I was struck by the positive attitude she had about her mastectomy. I rationalized that the loss of a breast must have seemed like so little to one who had lost her innocence far too early in life.

I was wrong. Joyce traded innocence for a premature awareness that self-dignity and self-love do not necessarily depend on how well we are loved or protected in our lives. Joyce chooses to define herself by what she contributes to the universe. She has spent her life in service to people, and the impact she has had on others is a testament to who she is and what she is about. The love she creates comes from a place that no surgeon's knife can take away.

My daughter came home one day in 1999 and announced that she had decided to raise $1,700 for the Whitman Walker AIDS Clinic and to run in the Marine Corps Marathon. My daughter is neither a runner nor an athlete. Instead, she is a woman with a clear vision for her life, based on a humanity that is fierce and unrelenting. She is a steamroller for human dignity, and her stand for it echoed with each pound of her feet against concrete. Inspired by Yael, I registered for the Avon Breast Cancer Walk, and I borrowed her running shoes to wear for the walk.

I walked to honor the courage of Miki and Joyce. I walked for all the women who could not walk on those days, or who would never walk again. I walked for the relatively healthy, able woman I am today and for the woman I could possibly be in the future who might not be capable of walking. I walked to raise funds and awareness for a disease that has taken too many lives. And I walked so that my daughter will never have to stop running.

I walked despite asthma and spinal surgery three years earlier that resulted in titanium rods being inserted down the length of my spine. I walked, carrying all of my fifty-two years with me. I walked every step, every mile. I walked with 2,800 others who brought the inspirations of their own Mikis and Joyces and Yaels to Frederick, Maryland that day.

I walked without foot discomfort, or injury. or real fatigue of any kind. It could not have been otherwise. Miki and Joyce guided my feet, every step, every mile. And I had the ultimate weapon to insure my success: I walked in my daughter's shoes.

JOYCE

"You have breast cancer." The dreaded words fell on my ears, and paralysis of my mind and body immediately set in. I could not hear anything after that. The doctor began to explain my options and what the next steps would be, but I remained frozen.

"You have breast cancer," continued ringing in my ears as my friend Marge helped me collect all the brochures and information the doctor was giving me to help me make a decision about a treatment plan. Everything felt unreal to me. *This* just could not be happening to me.

This cancer: the word, the disease, was like someone pointing a gun at me and threatening to pull the trigger. I was afraid that I was dying and that I had no control over the ravages of the disease, just like I had no control over the person with the gun pointed at me.

But this was happening to me. The year before, my mother was diagnosed with breast cancer and had undergone treatment just the way she does everything in life; with complete surrender, trust, and humor. She told all seven of us children that she wasn't ready to go, and we could just stop worrying. It hardly seemed possible that only one year later I was facing the same challenge. And, unlike my mother, I was filled with fear and dread. I was not convinced that I was going to live.

I spent most of that dark day crying. I cried for my fears: fear of the unknown, fear of pain, fear of dying, fear of loss of control, fear of disfigurement, fear, fear, fear, and more fear. I cried, too, for the anticipated loss of my breast, what I thought was a betrayal by my body, the confirmation that I was old and unworthy, all worn out and with no where to go in my life. Was this the end for me? Is this all that I had come to? I was more scared for myself than I had ever been in my life.

That same evening, my dear friend Jahn said something to me that was a catalyst to begin looking beyond my fears. She talked about possibilities that might come from my experience of cancer, that this might be an opportunity for me to be healthy. I wasn't sure what she meant by that. How could I be healthy when I had cancer? What did I have to look forward to? How much control and input did I have on the outcome of this chapter in my life? Did I have any control? She was suggesting that cancer was here in my life as an opportunity to live as opposed to a sentence to die.

As I look back on that day and the ones that followed, I know I did not fully understand and appreciate my friend's suggestion until months later. But she planted the thought, and I never forgot it as I began my cancer treatment process. Her words gave me some hope. And little did I know that my cancer treatment was the beginning of a journey that was a life treatment process!

To overcome my paralysis and avoid thinking too much about having cancer, I began doing what is standard operating procedure for me when facing a crisis: I got busy doing things. In this case, I started researching breast cancer to become knowledgeable on the subject. Oh, sure, I knew a good deal about it from my mother's experience the year before. But this was *my* breast cancer, and I wanted to know more.

I talked at length with my mother about her experience. Unlike my cancer, hers was a fast-growing cancer that was detected early through her annual mammogram. Mine had already spread from the duct into the surrounding area. My mother elected to have a lumpectomy followed by radiation treatment. I knew that she had experienced a great deal of fatigue and some burns during radiation. When I asked her about the lumpectomy, she told me that if she had to do it again she would elect a mastectomy. She felt disfigured with the lumpectomy.

Other friends, survivors of breast cancer, shared their experiences with me. At the same time, I read as much as I could process about the disease, treatments, and outcomes. A friend recommended Dr. Susan Love's *The Breast Book*, a virtual encyclopedia of information on the breast and all of its phases and functions. Two of my dearest friends, Judy and Virginia, whisked me off to Ocean City, Maryland, where I rested and read to make up my mind about what I wanted to do: lumpectomy or mastectomy, radiation or not. Chemotherapy could be decided later. I had less than a week to decide because the doctor cautioned me that there was no time to waste.

At the same time I was looking at my choices to determine the best options, I shared with others the challenge I was facing. I have never been very good at hiding my feelings from other people, but that was not the reason I decided to disclose my breast cancer to the people I was closest to. I shared because I knew I needed all the support I could get. I don't mean day-to-day functional support. This was a matter of life and death. I needed emotional and spiritual support.

Spiritual support was paramount. Up until this time I had been taking my life for granted, believing I could continue indefinitely my unhealthy life style of smoking three packs of cigarettes a day, hardly sleeping, working 80 hours a week, and pretending that I didn't need anyone. I loved my work and being needed—teaching, community organizing, political campaigns, volunteer director of an HIV/AIDS organization, and the source of support for my family.

I had spent the better part of my life being a savior of the world so-to-speak. I gave little attention to myself and my lifestyle. There was little time for me. I was so busy serving others, doing, doing, doing, that I wouldn't have a clue about what I needed, if I had ever thought about it—which I didn't. This was where I was when I was diagnosed with cancer.

As I shared my challenge with breast cancer, I experienced something I had never taken in. I felt the depth of my family and friends' caring. My boss, a doctor and CEO of an HIV/AIDS agency, cried when I told him. My mother, brothers and sisters, and many of my friends, wept. They, too, were afraid that I would die. I could see it in their eyes and hear it in their voices. And they offered to assist and support me in countless ways. But most important to me, everyone prayed for me.

For the first time in my life, I felt love and support from everywhere and everyone. The day I went to the hospital to undergo my mastectomy, I floated on prayers and good wishes for my survival. It was one of the most amazing feelings of my life: love and total support surrounded me. It had always been there for me. It's just that up until that time I had never sensed the depth of people's love and caring for me the way I did at that moment.

As I went to the hospital a week after hearing the cancer diagnosis, I was getting a glimmer of the "opportunity" Jahn had revealed that evening. This life-threatening challenge was not just about physical healing. This was an opportunity to grow emotionally and spiritually in ways I never imagined. It was a hint of what was to come for me in my personal transformation: I knew for the first time in my life that I wanted to live.

I mourned the loss of my breast. It was very similar to losing my uterus to a hysterectomy in my forties. Yet there were also some distinct differences. The loss of my uterus was not visible, and I no longer needed it for childbearing. It had outlived its function. Once I got used to the idea of losing it, I liked the idea of no longer experiencing difficult and profuse menstrual periods. I loved the idea, too, that I could no longer get pregnant. As I was moving through various affairs with men, it was something I did not have to worry about.

Losing my breast was very different. I loved my breasts and imagined that I would feel bereft, like half a woman. Yes, I was sacrificing my breast in order to save my life, but my breasts symbolized my femininity, they were a sexual turn-on, the outward manifestation of my womanhood. I was not only losing a breast, but I would be scarred, disfigured. I couldn't hide the loss of my breast like I could hide the loss of my uterus.

Once I chose to have a mastectomy, I waited anxiously to hear what the doctor found during my surgery, and then even longer to find out the lab results on my lymph nodes. Regardless of those lab results, I was told that I must stop hormone replacement therapy. Aargh! I had so loved HRT. I no longer suffered from the feeling I was on fire, even in the middle of winter, and sweating to the point that even the calves of my legs were dripping moisture! With HRT I had stopped waking in the middle of the night with night sweats that forced me to change my nightgown and sheets, and caused me to be constantly irritable and fatigued during my waking hours. Oh, how I hated giving up HRT.

My doctor said the lab results revealed my cancer was positive to estrogen. I did not have to undergo chemotherapy, but the doctor placed me on Tamoxifen. Not only did I have to give up HRT, but Tamoxifen assured that I'd get my hot flashes back because its job is to get rid of estrogen in the body.

Thus began my regression into the world of hot flashes, life filled with the inexplicable moments of turning red for no apparent reason. *Beware of combustible woman!* Those were not fun days, but when I was most irritable about the hot flashes, I remembered how thankful I was to be alive. I was recovering from the surgery. Now I was on my way! But to what?

During the months following my surgery, I experienced fear and anxiety, bordering on panic, whenever I felt a pain in any part of my body. I was sure the cancer had spread somewhere else. This is not a simple matter when you consider all the aches and pains of osteoarthritis, bad knees, weak ankles, headaches, indigestion, and gassy stomachs. All these perfectly normal ailments for the over-fifty set suddenly became possible new cancers.

After my scar healed, I was fitted for my first prosthesis and bras to hold it. I missed my cleavage terribly and had to make some adjustments in my wardrobe. The funniest thing that happened to me was when my prosthesis fell out of my bra when I bent over. I was trying out one of those wonderful push-up bras under a sweater. It looked good, a bit less matronly and much perkier. But alas, push-up bras aren't made to contain prostheses! Losing a boob in public can be quite embarrassing.

I also finally broke down and admitted that I wanted to be in a relationship, but secretly I was worried about how I would deal with my missing breast and the very apparent scar on my chest. Not to mention that I hadn't even been on a date in nearly ten years.

Like most women, no matter our age, I had had issues about my body and how it looked. I could never imagine how anyone would find it desirable. But now I was afraid I would truly horrify the poor man who ever dared to think of bedding me. While all these scary thoughts were racing through my mind every time I thought about the prospect of a relationship, newly found friends in Washington were urging me to date.

Nearly a year later, I met Andy, the man who became my lover and partner for five years. And wouldn't you know it, he was a breast man!

After several dates with Andy, we were necking in the car, trying to say good night, when I became aware that he was fondling my breast. I say that I became aware because I couldn't really feel anything. He didn't know that I had a prosthesis, so he thought he was fondling my breast. The situation was so funny to me that I burst out laughing. I imagine many men might be insulted at such a reaction, but not Andy. I explained that he was fondling a silicone prosthesis, which I'm sure feels like the real thing to the uninitiated. I assured him it did not turn me on.

When we finally made a date to make love for the first time, I was more than nervous. I wanted this man to enjoy me and me him. The funny thing is that my attempts to cover my scar lasted for about two minutes. In complete abandon, I let it all hang out. Later, Andy wanted to know what the big deal was. He said the scar wasn't anywhere near as bad as I made it out to be. But best of all, he said that my breast was so beautiful, the loveliest he had ever seen, and that one breast was better than most of the pairs of breasts he had seen! Andy confirmed for me that I was sexy and desirable, even with one breast. (Even if Andy was exaggerating a bit.)

It was pretty amazing to me what I was discovering about myself in the process of being in an intimate relationship. I was over fifty years old but feeling like I was twenty and in love.

There was a time, not too long after my mastectomy, that I thought about getting the other breast amputated to prevent the cancer from recurring. My doctor talked me out of that. And now I know that I would never want to give up this one remaining breast. I'm very attached to it! It gives me great pleasure.

Nothing changed and everything changed when I lost my left breast to cancer. I am still a woman filled with lust and desire, enjoying my body more than ever. I am filled with joy. I am whole. Nothing is missing. I am complete.

I got to treat my life in the process of treating my cancer. I happily traded a breast for an entire life. It was the best trade I ever made.

JEAN

Until April 2002, there was a certain distance between me and cancer, and I had little interest in exploring that space. No one in my family had ever had cancer. Joyce's breast cancer happened before I knew her. I was removed from the problem and saw no reason to learn about it.

Then, in April 2002, my younger sister Lynn found a lump in her breast.

Lynn went into the hospital to have a diagnostic lumpectomy. Mid-surgery the doctor came out to consult with her husband and me. The tumor was much larger than it had appeared to be: because it was flat and had ill-defined edges, it wasn't fully visible on the mammogram. There was no doubt that this was a large, malignant tumor. The doctor had sent a frozen section to the lab, and the results were back. Mastectomy was the way to go.

Lynn woke up missing one breast. I held her hand as she cried in shock and bewilderment.

> **Infiltrating ductal carcinoma** (IDC) begins in the milk ducts of the breast and penetrates the wall of the duct, invading the fatty tissue of the breast and possibly other regions of the body. IDC is the most common type of breast cancer, accounting for 80% of breast cancer diagnoses.

It makes my stomach queasy to read the words. This ugly *thing* had rocketed into my sister's life, and thus also into my consciousness.

Lynn was fifty-four years old and had stage three cancer. She was treated with nine months of very aggressive chemotherapy and six weeks of radiation. She was very sick for the last four months of the chemo. She couldn't get off the couch for weeks at a time. She had third-degree burns from the radiation. She had no hair. Her house, her business, and her husband's spirits went to hell.

At the end of her treatments, Lynn was declared to be in remission or NED: No Evidence of Disease. Beautiful words. They said it could take a year for her to recover from the chemo. Of course, they also said the chance of recurrence is fifty percent.

One month later my older sister Lois was diagnosed with breast cancer.

This was unthinkable. Two sisters, two cancers within ten months. Infiltrating ductal carcinoma. Lois's biopsy left no doubt, and again, mastectomy was the next move.

Lois had her mastectomy in February 2003 and then went through five months of chemotherapy. She got sicker for longer with each treatment. The final chemo left her weak and nauseated, with open sores in her mouth, and constant unpredictable diarrhea. Lois's husband had had stomach cancer the previous year, and she had nursed him through it, so he knew what she was experiencing.

Lois took the drug Arimidex for five years. She is now NED. Lynn was NED but could not take Arimidex or Tamoxifen. The drug she was taking to discourage recurrence was damaging her heart muscle. She was given a horrible choice: to continue the drug with probable serious heart damage; or, discontinue the drug and increase the chance of recurrence of the cancer. She gave up the drug. In June 2006, the breast cancer metasticized to Lynn's liver. She went back on extremely aggressive chemotherapy. To no avail. Lynn died September 6, 2006. She was fifty-eight years young.

This is a scourge that is on us. We are losing our mothers, sisters, daughters, and friends. Even if they are fortunate enough to live, horrible suffering is caused by the "cure."

There has been a determined and effective campaign to bring breast cancer to public attention and to stress early detection and survival. That is a good thing. Yet since we mostly hear only the stories about survivors in articles and TV ads and in the efforts to raise money for breast cancer research and prevention, we have not been educated about the horrors of the treatment. Vomiting, sores, diarrhea, rashes, nausea, bone aches, confusion, total exhaustion, and infections marked my sisters' courses of treatment.

Worse yet, we still don't know what causes breast cancer. After my two sisters were diagnosed, I joined The Sister Study, a National Institutes of Health study to find the environmental causes of breast cancer. I was desperate to do something to stop this disease that is robbing us of our sisters, and this was it. I became a consultant to the study, helping them recruit women over fifty to join it.

And then, in November 2005, my older daughter Jennifer was diagnosed with breast cancer. She found it herself through self-examination which she had begun after her aunts were diagnosed, so thank goodness it was very early stage. Jennifer had a lumpectomy and radiation, and her prognosis is very good. My younger daughter Lisa joined The Sister Study.

I am no longer distanced from breast cancer. I am now in the sisterhood, not because I have cancer, or because I have survived cancer. I simply have not *yet* had breast cancer. And that is the state of all women over fifty. We simply have not *yet* had cancer. But it is very possible that we will.

Most of us are temporarily two-breasted and able-bodied. I now know that not to learn about breast cancer, its causes, risk factors, progression and treatment, was simply my refusal to face reality. Our fears are realistic. In 2003, a quarter of a million women were diagnosed with breast cancer. Between ages forty and fifty-nine, one in twenty-four women can expect to get breast cancer.

And I have learned something even more important than the facts. When my sister Lynn was diagnosed, she was horrified. She resented every part of having cancer and viewed her body as having betrayed her. She had few close women friends, and none of them had experienced breast cancer. She could not come to any understanding or acceptance of what had happened to her. She suffered incredible psychological pain.

Lois, in contrast, had an amazingly peaceful reaction to the diagnosis. I asked her about it. She said that she was not at all surprised by her diagnosis. She knew the statistics. She said she always had had the position that "there is no reason why I should not get breast cancer." She had a group of female friends, a considerable number of whom had breast cancer themselves. They were already in place to support her and normalize her situation by the commonality of it. Her surrender to the possibility of having cancer, and her built-in support, made her entire course of treatment far less traumatic, and far less life-disturbing, than sister Lynn's.

There is no way to be comfortable with the fact of breast cancer. I know now, however, that determined ignorance about it is not my choice anymore. My eyes are open. I am sixty-six years old, and I have breast cancer in my immediate family. I am a candidate.

YOUR TURN

Discussion Questions:

1. If you have had breast cancer, how has it changed your life? Do you have fears of recurring illness? How do you cope with those fears?

2. If you had breast cancer and a mastectomy, do you feel sexual without your breast(s)? How, if at all, has the mastectomy affected your sex life?

3. If someone close to you has had breast cancer, how did you respond? How did you support the person?

4. If you have not had breast cancer, do you take all recommended steps for early detection? If not, why not?

Individual Exercise: *Share the Experience*

1. Call or visit two women who have had breast cancer. Do this exercise even if you yourself have had breast cancer. Request permission to ask them questions about their experience.

2. Ask first about the facts of their experience: when the cancer was discovered, what the diagnosis was (what kind of cancer and where located, etc), what the treatment consisted of, how long the treatment lasted, what effects the treatment had on their bodies.

3. Then ask them to describe their emotional journey, and sit back and listen. Ask them what type of support they had from friends or family during the experience, and whether they had wished for more or different support. Finally, ask what they learned about themselves through the experience.

4. For the next few days, think about what you heard, and what you learned. Then write a thank-you note to each woman to acknowledge her for sharing her story with you, and share with her what you have learned by talking to her.

Group Exercise: *Empathize*

The group will need a timekeeper for this exercise.

1. Visualize that you have just been diagnosed with breast cancer. See yourself in the doctor's office just after you hear the news. Notice your thoughts and reactions. What do you think? What do you say? Whom do you tell? Whom don't you tell? What will change in your life?

2. Respond to the above questions in your journal. You have five minutes to write. Begin your writing with "If I just found out I had breast cancer…"

3. Come back together as a group and discuss your experience.

Assignment:

Pretend you are the fourth author of *Saving the Best for Last* and write your story about "The Realities of Breast Cancer" in your notebook.

Solitude Versus Loneliness

We are social animals. From the moment of birth, we are part of a family that, for better or worse, defines who we are. When we become old enough to reach beyond the confines of our families, we start connecting with others at a rapid-fire rate. We fill our lives with as many people as possible. We often measure our success in life by how wanted we are, by how many people like us, by how adept we are socially. We win the game of life by having a standing-room-only funeral.

Loneliness, for many of us, is something to be avoided at all costs. If we surround ourselves with people, we will avoid it. Yet increasingly, many of us may experience the very feeling we are trying to avoid and wonder how this is possible. Others of us may feel uncomfortable when we are alone or if our social calendar isn't full. If we get home and have no voice mail, we may go into a tailspin.

Nowhere in our culture is the experience of solitude taught or valued. There are courses on Winning Friends and Influencing People, but where are the courses on Creating Solitude? When did we forget that we are our own company, that our inner world needs as much exploration as our outer world? When did we forget that we *have* an inner world?

Loneliness in the midst of people, even people we love, simply means that we aren't *connecting*. It isn't a signal to find *new* people but instead to reconnect with *ourselves,* first. Solitude is a way to find our center, to explore our inner world,, and to take as much nourishment and delight from our inner world as we do from our outer world. It's not easy. It means taking the time to be with ourselves and to resist reaching for the phone or the car keys in an attempt to connect with others. We may give up an afternoon with a friend, but we will reap endless rewards in another area. And we may discover that one of the wisest, funniest, or most interesting person we know is the one who shares our toothbrush each morning.

RENEE

I am an only child. I remember how frustrated I was growing up when my house was so quiet, and I had no one to talk to. From an early age, I sought out other children. I went to many sleepovers or wanted my friends to sleep over my house. I hated being alone. I remember having chicken pox and being told I couldn't be around other children for a week or two. Far worse than the itching was the loneliness. For hours, I sat in the open doorway of my house and watched other children play.

I always thought of loneliness as the empty and hopeless feeling that resulted from being physically removed from others. As a child, I recall crying at the sight of a man standing alone outside a store. People dining alone in restaurants always depressed me. My great-aunt lived alone for years, and I could not accept that she lived alone out of choice. The only way I could rationalize her living alone was to believe that no one wanted to live with her.

During the years of my marriage, I developed an appreciation of being alone, at least for short periods of time. In a world of husband, three children, and dog, even an hour to myself was a luxury. But the thought of living alone was different.

When my husband and I separated, I still had teenage children living at home. When the youngest went off to college, the middle one who had graduated came back for several years. When she left, the oldest one came back for awhile. After a year, he left. At the age of fifty-four, I was alone for the first time in my life.

What we all anticipated was that they would leave and my life would quietly settle into something less than it was before. "Will you be okay?" they asked as one by one they stood on my front porch, with their belonging-laden cars parked out front. "I'll be fine," I answered, because I knew that was the only acceptable answer for them. I don't think any of them believed me.

But what I discovered was that I *was* fine. The satisfaction of those small moments of being alone in past years didn't diminish now as the moments turned into hours and the hours into days. I was living alone, and I was actually happy.

When I began to date again after my divorce, I enjoyed having total freedom, although I was slightly surprised each time I was out late at night or staying at my then boyfriend's house that there was no one at home I had to call and check in with. ~~with~~.

My independence soared. I was proud that when it snowed, I was usually the first person on the block to go outside and shovel. I managed to deal with water pouring through my dining room ceiling, a dead furnace in winter, and the discovery of my cat in the family room, crouched under the TV table, clenching the hind half of a large squirrel in her jaws.

In May 2006, I remarried. I obtained a life partner and a housemate without losing any of my independence. About the only thing that has changed is that I defer to my husband in matters of snow shoveling. Since I've already made my point with myself about my ability to shovel snow, I can now graciously retire from the task.

Loneliness implies scarcity, an absence of connection. The years since fifty have allowed me a certain amount of reflection and subsequent insights about myself, and I now realize that for most of my life, I have actually experienced loneliness less when I have been physically alone than when I have been with others.

I give most people the impression of being a happy extrovert, and for years I believed myself to be an extrovert. People fascinate me. I love to use my sense of humor to entertain the people I'm around. I have always treasured the many friendships I've had over the years.

But I also discovered that there is another side to me. I often tend to mentally set myself apart when I am around others, even with my closest friends. I believe that others are always less complicated, that they are able to interact with each other without the constant stream of judgments, jealousies, and self-doubts like the ones that I often carry around in my head. As much as I do enjoy the company of others, I often find myself tuning out what is going on around me because the "noise" in my head is louder.

The noise quiets in my time alone, when I release myself from the fears that keep the wall up between me and others. I believe this "noise" will lessen as I continue to feel a sense of solitude when I am alone, a solitude I am experiencing for the first time in my life since turning fifty. In this newly-discovered solitude, I am able to draw richness from within, and the self-awareness I gain enriches my time and relationships with others as the noisy comparisons of lack and judgments I create in my head dispel.

Solitude sustains me in other ways as well. I like to be with myself and am rarely bored with my own thoughts. I enjoy the long journey inward, from which I bring back memories and insights both for my life and for the novels and short stories that I write. In solitude, my thoughts are abundant and clear. I don't have to search for answers. The answers are there waiting for me. There is peace.

JOYCE

I was lonely as a young girl who carried secrets too terrible to share with anyone. In my teens, I lived with thoughts of suicide as the only way to escape my mental prison. I felt alone and lonely even as I existed in a crowded household of ten people.

In my adult life, loneliness has not been a habitual experience. I am aware of feeling lonely only when I isolate and withhold myself from others. I usually disconnect when I feel needy, need assistance, or do not want to communicate something I fear will cause conflict.

Sometimes I still cut myself off from others because I have somewhat unconsciously believed for most of my life that I had to take care of myself and couldn't depend on others. I began early forging a persona of togetherness and competence. Asking for help didn't fit with my image, thus making it easy for me to isolate. Now I try not to make myself feel alone, but lifelong habits and ways of thinking do not go away. I must always try to stay aware of what I am doing.

My personality profile is that of an extrovert. I get much of my energy from relationships and interactions with friends, family, and coworkers, and spend many hours every week working, playing, talking, and socializing with others. I live in a congested, crowded area of the country. As a result of all this interacting, I crave time alone.

I became aware of this need years ago. After my divorce, my ex-husband and I each had the children every other weekend. On the Fridays when he picked them up at school, I would leave my job, get a special carryout meal, go home, turn off the phone, and eat while reading a good book. I loved the quiet, no demands for my attention, no need to talk, and I could indulge myself in whatever I chose. This arrangement was ideal, and I reveled in my time alone.

This time alone became solitude: a place of peaceful stillness, my time to give to me. Solitude allows me to listen to my thoughts and create without interruption. I can choose to do any of the many things I enjoy by myself. I love to eat alone, read, watch baseball, write, research, play computer games, go to the movies, take a walk, go shopping, or get in the car and go for a drive. I especially enjoy driving alone. It was one of my favorite escapes to get alone time when the kids were young, and I grew to relish long trips by myself. I've even driven across the country alone, and would delight in doing it again.

My need for solitude grew in my fifties. When I lived with others, such as when I was living with Andy, creating alone time for myself enabled me to maintain my equilibrium. Otherwise I felt smothered and drained of energy. If I have too much on my plate, or too many interactions with people, I feel off-balance, stressed, and a bit crazed. That's when I know I need to be separate for awhile.

In my sixties, owning my own welcoming, bright, airy condo creates a space for solace. Floor to ceiling windows give me a lovely view of a park and roaring stream, and I am wrapped in the pervasive quiet at the top of my high-rise. Many mornings I wake to the beauty of sunrise and stillness of the city. I get to feast on nature, even when I don't go outside. I rarely turn on the radio or television, and often do not play music. I do not want to be entertained. I simply luxuriate in being with myself.

Living in the city gives me the convenience of being close to amenities and work, but taking trips out of the city to beautiful places allows me to escape and renew myself. I appreciate landscapes and seascapes. As I breathe them in with all of my senses, I reconnect with my god spirit and experience solitude. I am replenished.

Solitude nurtures my spirit, boosts my energy, and gives me the ability to enjoy my relationships with others. Solitude allows me to withdraw and then to reconnect.

JEAN

When my first child was born, I was twenty-one years old. I was hundreds of miles from my parents and my sisters. I was lonely. I was so lonely I wanted to run away.

I was married for twelve years. When I was in the last years of my marriage, I was lonely. My children were there, and I had friends, but I was lonely.

Loneliness is an awful state. Hollow, transparent, without substance. When I am lonely, I feel invisible, even to myself. Loneliness is not related to where I am, what I am doing, or the number of people who are around. Loneliness is when my heart feels unsupported. Loneliness is when I feel that no one will be there with me in hard times. Loneliness is when I feel unloved, uncared for.

I felt lonely often in my thirties and forties, but far less so now. I have come to realize that it is my decision whether to be lonely. Loneliness is when I have shut myself off from sources of support. If I don't trust myself and don't trust others, I am lonely.

Over the past few years, as my spiritual practice increased, the occasions of loneliness decreased. I still get lonely, and when it happens, I roll around in it for a little while, and then I look to see the cause. Usually the cause is that I've been nurturing some feelings of inadequacy: maybe because I didn't get a mother's day card from one child; maybe because there was a poor response to the workshop I gave; or, maybe because I slighted a friend. I find the cause, forgive myself and others, and go on.

Also through my spiritual practice in the last few years, I have developed a taste for solitude. Solitude is nothing like loneliness. Creating solitude is an action, not a reaction. It is what I often choose, more and more since I turned fifty. Solitude is where I investigate what is in my heart. It is where I create my life. Solitude is where I commune with myself and my gods. In solitude, I am alone and silent.

Four years ago, I began attending a silent retreat once or twice a year. The retreats are held at a monastery surrounded by woods and fields and bordered by a river. There is a meditation path to walk. For two days, I speak to no one. I turn off my cell phone. I bring one book to aid my meditations and a pad and pen to write in a journal in the mornings. Otherwise, anything I normally use to distract myself stays home. I sleep in a 5' x 4' cell, with a cot, sink, desk, and chair.

At the first silent retreat, I thought I would die if I couldn't speak. Every time I passed someone in the hall, or sat down at their table to eat, words sprang to the front of my mouth. "Hey, how are you?" "Did you get to see the river?" "Does your room have one of those crucifixes on the wall?" "Whew, hot, isn't it?" "What do you do?" "Let me tell you about me."

As I observed my own tendencies, the sure knowledge grew that most of what I said in the normal course of a day was simply not necessary. My chatter added nothing to the world. And, as I got over my panic at having nothing to "do" at the retreats, and not having the release of chatter, I became calmer and more appreciative of the world around me. I began rising at dawn to watch the deer come out of the woods to graze in the field. I came to appreciate how much can be communicated by simply acknowledging someone with your eyes as you pass by.

Solitude is a gift. It is a gift that is given to us as we get older so that we might live fully, happily, and peacefully no matter what our life circumstances. It is a reward after all the years of "trying." It is a sweet treat at the end of the day. It is a secret pleasure. It is the bonus that was always there, if we had only known. It is God's gift.

YOUR TURN
Discussion Questions:
1. What is solitude? What is loneliness? Is there a difference for you?
2. Does either solitude or loneliness increase as you age? Which? Why?
3. Do you appreciate/crave solitude more as you age?
4. Are you ever lonely? Are you lonely when other people are around? What causes your sense of loneliness? What steps can you take to decrease loneliness?

Individual Exercises: *Practicing Solitude*
1. Create a half day where you make no plans, no commitments. Prepare for the day in several ways.
   - Tell friends you will be unavailable.
   - Gather your supplies: your favorite spiritual book, a notebook and pens, a beautiful plant or flowers, any favorite letters or cards you have received.
   - Have healthy, tasty food on hand for a snack.
   - Turn off telephones, televisions, Blackberrys, and computers. If you need to leave home to accomplish being alone and not speaking, do so.
2. Spend four hours by yourself.
   - Do not speak.
   - Write at least three pages in your journal about your feelings, fears, and expectations of your time alone.
   - Spend at least twenty minutes in meditation, broken up, if you wish, into two ten minute sessions.
   - Take one hour to go outside (weather permitting). Find a spot where you can look at beauty. Bring home something from nature—a leaf, stone, whatever strikes you. If you cannot go outside, or there is no physical beauty where you live (how awful), then concentrate on the flowers or plants you have in your home. Look at each leaf: its shape, color, construction. Look at the stems and the flowers. Admire them.
   - In your notebook, write what it is you like, or admire, or are drawn to about the object. Think about those same qualities

in connection with you. Do you have these same qualities? What is your commitment to having these qualities?

- During the rest of your time, read your spiritual book, meditate, and think about those you love.

- Before the end of your time of solitude, describe in your notebook what this time meant to you. Did anything frighten you? What did you learn? What did you think about? What did you dream about?

3. Finally, promise yourself to come back to the place of solitude whenever you wish.

Group Exercise: *Making the Choice Between Solitude and Loneliness*

For this exercise, you need a chalkboard, flip chart, or something to write on for everyone to see.

1. Go around the room and ask each person for a word or phrase that describes the state of solitude.

2. Go around again, asking each person for a word or phrase that describes the state of loneliness.

3. Discuss the differences between the two states. Discuss what in your life triggers loneliness. Does anything trigger solitude? If loneliness is a reaction, and solitude is a choice, can we choose solitude over loneliness?

Assignment:

Pretend you are the fourth author of *Saving the Best for Last* and write your story about "Solitude Versus Loneliness" in your notebook.

Rational Women Repeating Irrational Patterns

From time immemorial, women have been the bearers and guardians of children. It's easy to see that because of women's roles, they had to develop traits of steadfastness, loyalty, and the desire to nurture and protect. By having a male as part of the family unit, food and protection were often assured, and mothers could spend more time caring for and interacting with their young. Needless-to-say, keeping that male was of primary importance.

In today's world, we no longer need men to protect us or drag home large dead animals to keep us alive. But many of the traits we developed over hundreds of thousands of years have endured. We continue, even in the absence of predator wolves and enemy tribes, to believe that we cannot survive without our man.

We say "But I love him" as a way to explain physical or mental abuse. We believe that if we are loving enough, giving enough, thin enough, sexy enough, our partners will be the good, loving, decent people we know exist deep down. We go through one or ten relationships in the same way. Each time, our partner may have a different face, a different name, a different job. But he is the same man, and the end result is the same. We give ourselves away in pieces to make something work that doesn't work. And then we move on to the next "possibility."

We are often smart, accomplished, and in other areas of our lives, self-confident. So what is it that happens when we are face-to-face with a man with whom we feel a deep attraction? In many cases, we become someone we believe that man wants, rather than who we are. What is it that has us abandon ourselves and create something artificial? And, to put it another way, what is it that has us ignore the fact that this man was attracted to us in the first place and decide to become someone *other* than that person?

And what is it that has us enter into relationships with men who are simply on a different path than we are? We may want marriage and/ or children, and they make it clear that they do not. We may want to spend retirement years in travel, and they think a trip from the couch to the refrigerator is travel enough. We may have found someone who is kind, considerate, loving, and sexy, but who is simply not interested in the same kind of life we are.

Like many women, we three have had our share of failed relationships. And, like many women, our first reaction was that that the fault was with the men. Gradually, we came to the hard realization that the responsibility for the failure belonged to us. We had made choices that weren't compatible with our values or beliefs. We had lost ourselves in the relationships. We had traded our visions for our lives for a false sense of security.

We can't do anything to resurrect the past. But we can acknowledge that relationships with others are merely an extension of our primary relationship, the one we have with ourselves. That is the relationship that must be healthy if we are ever to make healthy choices.

RENEE

From age twelve on, my goal was to fall in love and get married and have children and live a perfect life. I knew I shared that goal with countless other females. There were two complications to my plan. The first was that my religious, observant parents expected me to marry someone Jewish, and I was rarely attracted to Jewish boys. The second was that I was afraid of boys and was very awkward around them. I couldn't imagine being the kind of person boys would be attracted to.

My first boyfriend became the man I would marry. He was Methodist and came from a family active in the church. After the initial shock, anger and frustration of various members of my family (my father said I was putting a knife in his heart), my parents reluctantly went along with my choice, all the while letting me know that they believed our chances of having a successful marriage were slim-to- none.

My goal then became not only to have a good marriage, but also to have a perfect marriage. Not only would my husband and I live happily-ever-after, the bonus would be proving that being a member of my family didn't doom me to a dysfunctional, neurotic life. I would prove that my family's prediction about my marriage was wrong. I would prove it wrong at any cost. I would have a life that bore no resemblance to the narrow-minded, over-protective way in which I was raised.

For a long time, proving my family wrong was easy. I was in love, and I considered my husband to be my best friend. My reaction to any discord in my marriage was to pretend it didn't happen. The first event that served as a model for countless others happened during our second year of marriage. I was cold, and so I turned up the thermostat. My husband noticed the rise in temperature and told me never to touch the thermostat again. If I was cold, I could put on a sweater. Case closed. I chose to comply, to stuff my mental arguments somewhere and not think about them. I saw my marriage as perfect, period. My family saw what I chose to present to them. And, because my marital problems had nothing to do with religious differences, I still felt vindicated where my family was concerned.

As the issues of control became more serious, my relationship with my husband felt more like that of a father and child than a marriage of equal partners. I had a decision to make. I could confront my husband and let him know how unhappy I was and ask him to work on the marriage with me, but taking such a path would be risky. I was afraid that if my husband knew how unhappy I was, he would divorce me rather than expend any energy on marital counseling. There would go my carefully constructed "perfect" life. I believed that no other man would want me, that I would be doomed to spend the rest of my life alone and unloved.

The decision I went with instead was to detach emotionally. It was so much easier to go along, to keep up appearances, to skim the surface of my life. It surprised me that my husband never seemed to be aware of my detachment. Neither did our friends or our children. Detachment eventually led to my being unfaithful, thereby resulting in the very consequences I had feared: my marriage ended. I was 46 years old.

I was terrified at the prospect of living life alone. Since age twenty-two, I had been Mrs. Someone, living Mrs. Someone's Big Secure

Life. My husband and I were educated, affluent, worldly, and non-religious. My married life had been a complete change from the way I was raised.

Without that, I didn't know who I was anymore. Worse, I believed I was no one. When I looked in the mirror, nothing looked back. When I moved out of my marital residence, I spent years in a kind of limbo. I bought a house and lived in it without furniture. I returned each morning to my marital residence, drank coffee and read the newspaper with my husband as usual, did the laundry there, and once even cleaned the house when he was going to have a party for people at the office. I didn't tell my family about the separation. Distance and infrequent visits worked in my favor.

My overwhelming feeling was that my life had shifted from forward motion to a state of suspension. The sensation was that of being on a treadmill, with the same thoughts circulating through my head thousands of times a day. The extra-marital relationship I had been in continued, a relationship that I knew was unhealthy, but I was incapable of ending.

From an early age, I had two competing views that controlled my life: deference to the needs of others and self-centeredness. My mother was my role model for adversity with a "don't react, don't argue, don't make waves" policy. I adhered to the same policy. I was also raised as the center of my family's universe as an only child and the only child of two grandparents. I was constantly praised and could do no wrong.

These beliefs created conflicting behaviors in me. Outwardly, I never expressed anger at anyone. I suppressed negative feelings, and they festered for weeks, months, or forever. I always wanted everyone to like me, and so I would say or do whatever I thought would achieve that end. On the inside, I had constant judgments about people, mostly stemming from my exacting "how it should be" rules that I made up about how people should be. My way of reacting to all this was to dwell obsessively and remain silent: a terrible, strangling kind of silence that ate away at me.

At age forty-nine, I enrolled in workshops that were geared to help people identify their goals and give them the tools to achieve them. On the registration card, I was asked to write what I wanted to get out of the workshops. I wrote, "I don't want to be crazy." The workshops showed me how to step back and look at my life and see what wasn't working and why. I discovered I had the capacity within myself to make different choices. Most important of all, I was able to forever dispel the notion that I was a victim to my own life.

For years I had dreaded losing the perfect marriage. I was now able to see that the "perfect marriage" never existed. If I lost anything during those years, it was my commitment to my relationship and my courage to take a stand for the life I wanted. Had I admitted that at the time, there could have been an opening to work on my marriage and make it healthy or, at the very least, a way to end it with integrity.

In the years since turning fifty, I have become more independent and self- assured than I have ever been before. When I was fifty-five, I met Dan, a good, decent man and we created a loving relationship.. On several occasions, we informally discussed the possibility of living together. Those discussions triggered in me a nagging fear that if I ever did decide to live with a man again, I might repeat the same patterns of my marriage. I might defer, accommodate, and avoid confrontation. I might lose myself. And I never wanted to lose myself again.

I made a personal commitment to stay true to myself. Being true to myself means being true to the commitments that are important to me: my children; my friends; my career; my creative pursuits, and my self-reliance. This is what creates my sense of self. As much as I have the need to be liked, accepted, and loved, I will not give up myself in order to fill that need. I will give up a relationship rather than give up myself.

In 2006, at the age of fifty-eight, I married Dan. Since then, I have made good on my commitment. I am happy because I make *myself* so. I am fulfilled because I fulfill *myself.* Nobody has the ability to complete me; I complete myself. I am with Dan not because I need him but because I choose to be with him. My relationship is happy, healthy, loving, and supportive, not because I found the "perfect" man, but because I became the "perfect" woman.

JOYCE

When I decided to move into my boyfriend Andy's house (so weird to say "boyfriend" at age sixty-six), I was looking forward to creating a life together. When I asked him if I could move in, he readily agreed. Since I had dated Andy for two years before moving in, there wasn't much I did not know about him.

My experience of Andy had been his unconditional acceptance of me. He never tried to change me despite our major differences in background, lifestyle, and political beliefs. We enjoyed friendly, warm relationships with our children, siblings, and exes. He's a very funny, smart, and likeable guy. He is a man of his word. It was easy to fall in love with him.

I also knew that living with him would be a difficult adjustment. Andy spends much of his time building his collections of music, books, videos, and antique toys. Nearly every square inch of his house overflows with treasures he's been amassing for over twenty years, together with family heirlooms and household items inherited after each of the deaths of his parents, uncle, and cousin. He loves his pictures, posters, memorabilia, and shelves of model cars and trucks that cover every square inch of every wall of his house. There is also a television in every room.

I am a creature of order. I like wide-open spaces, cleanliness, light, greenery. I do not collect anything. In fact, I usually clean out and give away anything I have not used in the previous six months. I also like my space to be quiet. I watch television only two or three times a year and then only if I can get a baseball game from Baltimore.

After I moved in, it took me months to get Andy to clear one room of his belongings so that I could have my own office. I had the room painted and bought new office furniture. I stuffed my considerable wardrobe into the one tiny closet in that same room and moved all my other possessions into the same crowded space. Unfortunately, Andy's bookcase with all the National Geographics printed in the twentieth century took up a lot of space in my tiny, crowded room, but he refused to remove them. The room never really became mine.

After two years, I found myself dreading returning to Andy's house. When I was at the house, I didn't want to be there. For me it was not an inviting, warm, and comfortable living space: it had not become my home. Andy owned the house, and I lived there.

My reason for moving in with him was that I loved him and hoped we would create a future together. Falling in love can happen at fifty-something, and it happened to me. I was convinced that I wanted to marry this man. I knew without question that he and I have very different needs about space and organization, yet I made my decision to move in with him under the delusion that love, my love, would carry the day. Andy would be so happy living with me that we would negotiate our living habits and partner to create a home that both of us could enjoy.

In spite of all I have learned about myself, my heightened awareness of what is important to me, I fell into a lifelong trap that many women fall into: the delusion that if I love a man enough, he will magically change in the way I want him to.

I know now that I had a vision for our lives that Andy did not share. We never sat down and created shared goals. I ignored all the red flags. Whenever I said I wanted to be married to him, he would repeat that he was happy with our relationship the way it was. Did we really need to change it? I didn't want to push him, or rock the boat too much, so I let it go. I continued to believe that my love would change all that.

The final brick to fall on my head occurred when I asked Andy to add an addendum to his will so that if anything happened to him, I would have a place to live until I could make other arrangements. My goal was not to inherit his house. I was simply looking ahead and acknowledging the critical fact that I owned no place to live. He said that his daughter would never put me out on the street and not to worry about it. I was surprised and hurt at his answer to my reasonable request. I did not ignore that red flag.

I did worry about it. I was living with a man in his house, a house over which I had no legal rights. If anything happened to him, technically I would not have a place to live. I needed to secure my future. Either he did not understand my concerns, or he did not *want* to understand. I chose not to challenge him or to make it a source of conflict, but it hurt so much that it woke me up: Andy was not going to change—period.

I told Andy I was moving out. The expression on his face indicated his hurt. As much as I could, I explained my reasoning in a non-judgmental way. I wanted him to understand that my decision to move had to do with making myself happy and giving myself future security.

I also pointed out to him that together we were no closer to a common vision for our lives than when I moved in.

I made it clear that I did not expect him to make me happy. While I assured him I did not want to end our relationship, I intended to buy a house that supported the way I wanted to live my life and the kind of environment I wanted to create. He told me I was impatient and that he was making changes in the house. Andy wanted me to stay, but by this time I knew better.

I recognized how unhappy I was living with Andy. I experienced enormous pain and disappointment with myself. I moved in with him with my eyes wide open, but somehow I thought he would be different after I moved in.

I cannot in fairness blame anything on Andy. He never misled me. I knew him, and I knew what made him happy. I was well aware of how he had chosen to live for the past twenty years. Further, I was the one who suggested moving in with him.

I found a beautiful condo close to Washington, D.C. As soon as I walked in the door, I knew I was home. The view from my living room and bedrooms was breathtaking. It overlooked Alexandria, with a park and stream directly in front of my building. My apartment was light, roomy, clean, spacious, uncluttered, quiet, and mine! Every time I came home, gratitude involuntarily spilled from my heart to my lips: "Thank you, thank you, thank you!"

After Andy and I separated, I rediscovered the elements of our relationship that I most appreciated. I enjoyed him so much more now that we were not living together. We made dates to spend time enjoying the things we love to do together, sometimes including dates to make love. We took a delightful vacation together. I experienced increased sexual attraction, and the sex was better—like it was when we first dated—lusty, spontaneous, exciting. I looked forward to our time together rather than dreading going home.

The process of getting to this place was painful. I wanted to avoid having to face the fact that living with Andy did not work for me. I did not want to admit it, or talk about it with my best friends. I reverted to thinking that revealing my thoughts to my friends would make me a failure in their eyes. Everyone I knew would think that I had made a big mistake. I felt distressed that at my age I had fallen into a pattern from my past.

When I finally admitted how I felt and talked about it, I was able to move away from my worries about what people thought. Then I was able to focus on what I wanted and needed.

Moving in with Andy was a blind error in judgment, but it was also an opportunity to grow and learn. It enabled me to know, yet again, what I want and that I cannot settle for less. I will not compromise my values and happiness, not even for love.

I gave up a domestic partnership in order to actualize my vision for my life. It was a powerful decision to move out—even in a bad situation it is difficult to reach for more or better. And in the end, I realized that I could not, and did not, lose what I didn't have.

JEAN

There are two beliefs deeply ingrained in many, if not most, heterosexual women born before 1960. The first is that without a life partner we are inadequate as women. The second is that to attract and keep a man we must subordinate our own personalities, wants, and aspirations, to his. These are two harmful beliefs. These beliefs lead us to be dishonest in relationships; and, should the relationships fail, they lead to our anger, guilt, and bitterness. "How could he leave/ betray/ mistreat me when I have given up so much for him?"

The fact is, we have "given him" everything but our true selves. The fear of failing this most basic of female "accomplishments," having and keeping a man, has led us to be insincere and inauthentic with our loves. My lesbian friends tell me that the conditioning is so strong that despite the fact that their partners are female, they engage in the same behaviors.

Upon my marriage at age twenty, I gave up any dreams of what I wanted to accomplish in the world. For that, I received approval all around. At twenty I did not have the imagination or courage to strike out on a new path.

Asserting my own desires for another purpose in life did not occur for another twelve years and then only after I made myself, my husband,

and my children, miserable. I swore to myself that from that time on, being true to myself would be the primary principle of my life.

By age thirty-five, I was typing the legal article my law school lover was writing to get onto the Law Review (law school's highest honor). This may not sound so ridiculous until you realize that I too was in law school, plus I was a single mother, plus I was working three jobs. I was not even attempting the Law Review competition myself because I couldn't fit it in with child care, classes, study, and work. He was attending law school courtesy of his parents. He had no jobs and no other responsibilities. He was getting "A's," I was getting "B's," and I was typing his paper. After all, I loved him.

My lover did not force me to type his paper. He didn't even ask me to do so. I offered. I offered to support my man at my sacrifice. My conditioning prevailed. He made it onto the Law Review. He broke up with me a few months later. I thought he discarded me for a younger woman. I was hurt and furious. I had given so much.

In the break-up process, he said something that I ignored at the time because it didn't fit my paradigm. He said, "I was attracted to you the first moment I saw you. You stood out as someone who was wholly herself and wholly confident. But something changed."

I nursed my hurt over his betrayal for years. I didn't see any connection between my behavior in my marriage and my behavior in this relationship. After all, I was now pursuing my dream. I was not that wimpy insecure young girl I had been in my marriage. Rather than using the painful experience to gain insight into myself, I began hardening my shell. The only way not to be hurt like that again was not to love wholly again. To me, that was the logical response to what had happened.

Then I met my next love. He was as much the opposite of me as possible. He was an ex-Vietnam Marine who ran a bar owned by his father. He had a ninth grade education and dressed like a cross between a hippy and a motorcycle gang member. He was handsome and virile. I thought I was safe with him because how could I possibly fall in love with such a man?

But I did, to the extent my then limited ability to love allowed, and the door was opened, yet again, to the old patterns of supporting my man by giving up pieces of myself. While the shape it took was different, and there were no legal papers to type, the experience and effect were the same. I molded myself to him. He was very jealous, so I cut out friendships with other men, then with old friends (male and female), and even with family. He was volatile, so I watched my words around him. We listened to his music, watched his movies, and participated in his favorite activities. Moment by moment, year by year, I disappeared.

He didn't force me into doing any of that. I did it. I did it for my man. I did it because it was expected by my useless, outdated vision of how the world is structured. I did it because I didn't want to lose yet another man. I did it because I was born in an era where such behavior was expected and defined success.

We were together for thirteen years. When we broke up, it was only because he had made life too intolerable even for me. I disliked him when we broke up, but I disliked myself even more. By this time, I saw the pattern. I saw how deeply ingrained it was in me to get a man and hold a man no matter what it took from me.

It has been over ten years since that relationship ended, and I have not had another serious relationship since. I have done a lot of work on myself, on my health, on my spirit.

I have thought a lot about how I act in romantic relationship and realize that I act differently than I do in all other relationships. In most of my life I am real, honest, connected, and filled with energy. But when even contemplating a romantic relationship, I separate that person from all others. He becomes "special" and I relate to him differently. Out the window goes honesty. In comes manipulation. I want to get him to like me, to be attracted to me.

I had a great example of this dynamic five years ago. I went on a two-week rafting trip through the Grand Canyon. I had never been rafting and was nervous and frightened. To take my mind off my fear, I decided to create real relationships with the other twenty-two people on the trip. I began to do that and started out each conversation by asking, "What is your vision for your life?" People responded with interest and enthusiasm. Many had never had such a conversation before. Those conversations were the beginnings of some wonderful, and still present, friendships.

Meanwhile, I was very attracted to one of the five guides, and I wanted him to be attracted to me. I didn't have the vision conversation with him. Instead, I posed prettily. I thought up and delivered clever opening conversational gambits. I hung around his orbit in hopes he would talk to me. All of these tactics bombed. Nothing worked. The man was indifferent to me.

On our last day on the river, I metaphorically threw in the towel. He just wasn't interested. He, in fact, seemed to avoid and dislike me. I gave up. Having given up, I went up to him at lunch and asked, "What is your vision for your life?"

Oh my goodness. The doors opened, the sun came out. He began talking and our conversation went on the entire night and well into the next day. He became my friend, and my romantic friend, and to this day we are in communication.

I glimpsed for the first time what a disservice I do others in the name of romance. I had cut him out of the herd for special treatment. In doing so, I made him less than others, and I made myself less than I am. I treated him as an objective rather than a human. I didn't relate, I plotted.

When a relationship begins dishonestly, it cannot become honest. When I begin a romantic relationship by "selling" myself, I will continue to "sell" myself throughout the relationship. No one ever "did" anything to me in a relationship. I sold myself out, and by doing so I sold out others. I now understand what my law school lover meant when he said, "I was attracted to you the first moment I saw you. You stood out as someone who was wholly herself and wholly confident. But something changed."

A friend told me that there are only two kinds of hearts, closed or open. A closed heart cannot give or receive love. An open heart can do so, but it also may be wounded. Not selling out and giving in to manipulation to attract and keep that special man means standing in integrity to create a lasting and healthy romantic partnership. A partner is not interested in only a piece of me, nor am I willing to be inauthentic or keep this aspect of my life separate. A painful lesson, but an honest lesson in respect for myself and others.

Old patterns die hard. I am not yet confident I am able to create and maintain a love relationship in which we can both be whole, tell the truth, support each other, and be willing, at any moment, to give the relationship up to maintain self-respect. But my commitment is to having such a relationship in my life, and so I will get there.

YOUR TURN
Discussion Questions:
1. What are the patterns you repeat in your relationships? Do these work for you? What do you want to change? Why?
2. Why do you think successful, independent women sometimes act needy and dependent with men?
3. If you áre partnered, are you aware of patterns in your relationship that don't serve you, but that you keep repeating? Explain. If you aren't partnered, are you aware of patterns in your past or present that prevent(ed) you from having the kind of relationship you would like to have?

Individual Exercises:
Exercise One: *Recognize Your Patterns*
1. If you feel you ever have compromised your essential self in order to preserve a relationship, describe in writing specifically how you did so and what you gave up. No one stays in any relationship without getting something out of it, so consider what you gained by staying in the relationship.
2. Was what you gained worth what you lost?
3. Was your partner aware of what you were giving up? Did your partner appreciate it? Have you behaved in this way in other relationships? How will this behavior stop?

Exercise Two: *Shift Your View*
1. Make a list of the qualities that are essential for you in a romantic partner. Have at least seven items on the list. Be specific when naming the qualities. So instead of "comfortable to be with," put what it is that constitutes "comfortable to be with" such as "kind," "relaxed," "sense of humor." **Do not read further until you have made the list**.
2. Have any of your romantic partners had all of the qualities? If they did not have the qualities, did you engage in the "he/she will change" fallacy? Did it work?
3. Now think about whether you yourself have the qualities you listed. If you do not have the qualities you require in a romantic partner, then how or why would a person with those qualities be attracted to you? And more importantly, then how could you love yourself?

Group Exercise: *Reorganize Your Patterns*

You will need a timekeeper for this exercise.

1. Form pairs. Pick a Partner A and a Partner B, and decide which partner will go first.
2. Think of the romantic relationships you have experienced in your life. Do not overlook your high school crushes.
3. Focus on and describe to your partner the ways in which the people you were involved with were alike. (For now, forget how they were different.) They may have been alike in how they treated you, or how the relationship ended, or how you had fun together, or who loved who more, or whatever.
4. Talk with your partner about why you think you might have chosen partners with these characteristics.
5. When both partners have completed the exercise, discuss with each other what your commitments are for present or future relationships.

Assignment:

Pretend you are the fourth author of *Saving the Best for Last* and write your story about "A Rational Woman Repeating Irrational Patterns" in your notebook.

Faith and Spirituality

In the deepest places of our being, we tend to look at meaning beyond ourselves. We may know that our life expectancy is a finite number of years, but this doesn't answer why we were put on earth to begin with. We may know that cellular deterioration will be how most of our lives will end, but this doesn't answer what, if anything, will come next.

Whether we identify ourselves with a religion, believe in the sanctity of nature, karma, reincarnation, or simply that we are all connected, we are all inclined to be spiritual beings. We are, with the greatest array of scientific discovery at our disposal, inclined to look to the heavens and wonder at the majesty of it all or suck in our breath at a plant beginning to bud, or marvel each year at the first snowfall. We are, in spite of an endless source of ever-increasing knowledge about conception, gestation, and birth, speechless at the moment of our children's or grandchildren's entry into the world. We are every bit as awe-struck as we were tens of thousands of years ago, when lightening streaked across the sky, or a baby sucked air into its lungs and screamed for the first time.

As many of us age, we cling more tightly to our faith, or discover it in a new way. We come to relish the journey of the soul with as much or more anticipation than we used to relish the accumulation of material goods or our hard won professional progress. In addition to listening to people's words, we learn to hear the silence. In addition to taking in the knowledge of others, we learn to listen to the wisdom within. And we understand that our world is only as rich as we believe it to be. We, who have been given the gift of experiencing midlife and beyond, become more humbled and awed daily by a universe that reveals itself in the grandest way possible and in the smallest.

RENEE

I'm a first-generation American-born Jew. My parents were born in Eastern Europe. I was accustomed to hearing only Yiddish spoken when we were at my grandparents' house. At our house, there was always a mixture of Yiddish and English. My father was kosher. My mother, in deference to her husband, maintained a kosher home.

My family observed all holidays strictly. The day before Passover, my mother put away our dishes and silver. Out came the special dishes and silver used only for the eight days of Passover. My mother even had special Passover pots, pans, and dish soap. We ate only kosher for Passover food.

My parents didn't have enough money to join a synagogue, so I was enrolled in religious school under my aunt and uncle's membership. I didn't understand why people needed money to worship. I didn't understand why I had to leave my home to pray to God. Weren't my nighttime prayers enough?

By the time I was in late elementary school, I was spending four days a week at the synagogue. I continued with my religious instruction until age sixteen when I was confirmed. For most of that time, I viewed my religious education as a necessary evil in my life. I experienced no personal connection to my religion.

For years, I debated whether to put my children through some kind of religious training. I felt that I would be insulting my family if I didn't. In the end, I decided I wanted them to know their heritage. I believed that whether they chose to follow any of the traditions of Judaism was up to them; but I felt that they needed the knowledge in order to make the choice.

While my children were connected to the temple through their religious studies, I was connected as well, if only in the most peripheral way. Since I had to be a temple member for my children to be enrolled in the religious school, I joined. I drove them to classes, and I supported them through the Bar and Bat Mitzvah process. My youngest son was Bar Mitzvahed when I was forty-nine years old. At the completion of his Bar Mitzvah, there was no longer any need to be a member of the temple. By age fifty, I had severed the ties.

I do not attend services, abide by dietary laws, or observe the Sabbath. I will always feel guilty about not following the religion that was so important to my family, as well as to the countless generations that preceded mine. But my rejection of the formal laws of Judaism doesn't mean that I would prefer instead to follow another religion. I simply don't feel comfortable with the notion of any organized religion.

When I was thirteen, I was introduced to the writings of Edgar Cayce, who, under hypnosis, was able to diagnose illness and prescribe their cures. While under hypnosis, he also answered questions about the meaning of life. Cayce spoke of humanity as a collection of souls, souls that incarnate multiple times until they reach a level of "perfection." I interpreted perfection to be the state of total giving, total peace, and total connection to the universe. I was comfortable with that view of life. It's a powerful concept, and it changed how I looked at the world.

I used to see people as finite, stamped by whatever color they wore on their skin or whatever life circumstance in which they were involved. I reacted to them by what was external. Now, if I think of them simply as souls, they lose their outer identity. They are of no specific race, religion, or economic circumstances. Their lives, like mine, are in the process of evolving. All of us have gifts, and all of us have the possibility to evolve to a higher level in this incarnation. Mother Theresa, for example, would be an example of a highly evolved soul. Those souls who harm others, who fail to use their lives as a positive force, will have future lifetimes in which to deal with the issues they have created in this lifetime.

When I use the word God, I am referring more to a universal energy source, rather than a deity. We souls are all part of the universal energy. And there is no time limit imposed. In my current incarnation, I carry my previous incarnations with me.

The rules or laws of a specific religion don't dictate my life. It's about using my abilities and my gifts to enhance the lives around me. If we are all evolving together, we all have a stake in each other. Every action, wherever it occurs, affects me. Each of my actions affects all others. We cannot underestimate the effects of our actions.

The best of any religion is that part which honors the dignity of life and instills in people a responsibility for the welfare of others. I try to live my life that way. For me, it's about being the best mother, the best friend, the best lover I can be. It's about serving my clients in the best way I know how and about writing fiction that will have an impact on people. It's about reminding myself everyday that I have a purpose for being here. It's about going to sleep each night knowing that I made a contribution each day.

My only nod to Judaism is my annual Passover Seder, to which I invite as many non-Jews as possible. For me, the Passover meal is simply a joyous gathering where we commemorate a people who chose freedom over slavery. The Seder is about human dignity and great food. I can't think of a better way to spend an evening.

JOYCE

When I was eight years old, my father moved the family to South Baltimore where an Evangelical United Brethren Church was four blocks from our house. We children went to Sunday school and church services every week or else were punished by my father.

I learned if one prayed to God, He would grant wishes. In my child's mind, I believed that if God answered my prayers, my father would be kind and I would be pretty. Since God did not do what I asked, I was confused. I wondered whether I didn't deserve to have my requests granted, I hadn't asked in a proper manner, God didn't acknowledge selfish wishes, or perhaps God wasn't listening at all.

My experience at Sunday school and church was confusing, too. On one hand, the Christian creed taught that everyone was equal in God's eyes, yet, I felt that church members treated my sisters, brothers, and me like outcasts. We were poor children who didn't dress and act like those from middle class homes. We were good kids, but we didn't fit in. It was one of my first experiences of stigma and discrimination.

As I got older, I began to realize, too, that the church I attended sent money overseas to missions to proselytize Christianity, while ignoring the poverty of the neighborhood. I also thought that was unfair.

My formative experience in organized religion confirmed my

inferiority in the world, but many Christian teachings took root in my heart and mind nonetheless. The golden rule, do unto others as you would have them do unto you, became a principle in my foundation of beliefs about how I should live my life. Being in service to others, or performing "good works," also took root from those early teachings.

At sixteen, I felt lost. My mother said she trusted me to make sound decisions and do the right thing. She seemed to think I was an adult, but I no longer had my moorings. I needed strict guidelines. I wanted someone to tell me what to do.

My closest friends were Catholic, so I began to attend Mass. I loved the rituals and ceremony of the Catholic Church. I appreciated the structure and strictness of its teachings and after taking lessons, I joined the Catholic Church at eighteen. I attended Mass nearly every day and went to confession, where the priest told me when I was committing a sin and to say my Hail Marys as penance. It gave me focus, it was something I could grasp, and I did not have to make decisions. The Church laid down the laws to live by.

I was frightened about my sexuality and passion. I was afraid to do anything that would fly in the face of God who I believed had protected me. I didn't want to do anything that might reflect a lack of gratitude. Many conflicting feelings and thoughts seemed to run my life, but I was able to adhere to the strict teachings of the Church.

My sense of God or a higher power grew within me. I counted my blessings every day: my father was gone; my family was surviving; I was pursuing my dream of becoming a teacher; and I had friends. I knew that I was lucky, thanks to God.

When my husband and I married in our twenties, we had a small ceremony in the Evangelical United Brethren Church. He was raised Catholic but had not been observing the practices or attending Mass for many years. We planned to put off having a family, but the Church's policy on birth control was contrary to what we wanted, so we began attending services at a local Presbyterian Church.

In the milieu of the 1960s I began to question all traditional beliefs, including the role of religion and politics in society. I questioned the need to belong to a church and after several years of soul searching, I reached the conclusion that organized religion no longer served me. I experienced faith and spirituality in many ways, most often when I was in a natural setting—the woods, near the ocean, in the mountains, or walking in a garden. Nature and being out of doors, unconfined, freed me from the strictures of buildings or doctrines. At that point in my life, I worshipped nature.

When our daughter and son were born, we had them baptized because it was a custom in my family; but baptism no longer had a religious meaning for me. As parents, my husband and I decided not to raise the children in any formal religion. We chose instead to expose them to many beliefs and cultures, just as we were exploring new thoughts on faith and learning about all world religions.

When the children were old enough, we attended meetings of the Theosophical Society, a non-dogmatic, non-religious organization where participants are encouraged to adopt ideas that make sense and are real and important to them. There is no creed; Theosophy is a simply a way of looking at life.

Through those meetings, reading many books over several decades, exploring astrology, and doing past life regressions, I came to believe in reincarnation and karma. I came to believe that we are here to evolve as human beings: if I don't learn my lessons in this life, I get to do them over in the next. Karma dictates that if I do harm or evil, I shall atone for it in my next life.

Now I refer to "God" by many names: God, Goddess, Creator, higher power, spirit, the Universe. I use all of these interchangeably. When I say God/He, it is an old habit. God is amorphous to me, an all-pervasive spirit. God resides in me, God is my soul.

During the past three decades, my spirituality and connection with the universe and God through nature has continued to grow. Communing with nature is one of the best ways to renew my spiritual connection with the universe. It grounds me and infuses me with energy, while at the same time I feel rested and at peace with myself.

I believe that the world and the people in it are basically good. I believe that we should treat the earth gently and respect the environment. I believe we are all connected. Whatever affects one affects all. Thus, whatever I put out into the universe comes back to me. My thoughts, like my prayers, go out into the universe and have the power to effect change.

Religion and my evolving faith and spirituality have confirmed my purpose in life: to be in service to others and to use my talents and abilities to contribute to the world. My prayers are mostly to give thanks. While I pray for certain things, I believe in the power of good works and taking action for what I believe to be true. I have the power to create, and thus I live by the saying from Mother Jones: "Pray for the dead, but fight like hell for the living."

JEAN

I was raised in the Dutch Reformed Church. My family went to Sunday school and church every Sunday. I was baptized and received my first communion at thirteen. My father was a deacon and then an elder in the church—the highest lay position in a local church. Despite appearances, religion was a very small part of our lives. Church was a big part; but religion, the idea of God, the idea of somehow living a faith-based life, was non-existent. I don't remember ever discussing any aspect of religion in our home. Church was church, school was school, and home was home. From my perspective, church was where you got some sort of measuring stick for your behavior, rather like the rules that governed behavior in school. But nowhere was there any feeling that anything I heard or saw or did in that setting had any connection with the core of my being. Actually, at that time, I didn't even know my being had a core.

God seemed to be an amorphous, vague figure who treated people like puppets. He tested Abraham by demanding he kill his son Isaac, then taking back his demand at the last minute. It seemed a bit sadistic to me. He killed the first-born son of all the Egyptians to make them free the Israelites. Why choose one people over another? Once he wiped out all people except one family in the great flood without a backward look. God acted out infrequently, however, so it didn't really worry me. Jesus, on the other hand, made me vaguely uncomfortable. He was soft and feminine. In his behavior, he was everything I could never be. And, I didn't understand anything he said.

In my teenage years, I remember being very jealous of my Catholic friends because they got to go to confession. To me, they had a direct tie between their personal behavior and God. They confessed, they repented, and they were forgiven. Now that kind of God I would have appreciated. My non-introspective mind and my clear sense of action-deserves-reaction mindset would have welcomed a God that helped me clear things out on a weekly basis.

I even went to a religious college. Attendance at chapel every morning was required, as was one class a year in religion. None of that, no sermons I heard, nothing I studied, nothing moved anything in me.

And finally, I married a man who became a minister. When he was in seminary, they had two classes for the wives of seminarians, both of which I dutifully attended. The first was "Theology Made Simple." The second was "What to Serve at Church Meetings in Your Home." We practiced making and serving hot chocolate.

All of this deeply offended me, but I did not then even recognize that feeling for what it was. This was the late 1950s, early 1960s. There was no women's normal. I seemed abnormal.

For twelve years, I was a minister's wife. I went to church, was the church organist, taught Sunday school, and attended the ladies' bible study. I was miserable but put on a good face because I had no explanation for my misery except my own shortcomings. I certainly never made any real connection between myself and anything bigger than myself.

I suspect that despite my best efforts, I wasn't a very good minister's wife. My skirts were too short, I laughed at the wrong times, I never visited the sick, my kids were dressed perfectly only for holidays, and I swore.

In my early thirties, after twelve years of marriage, I was divorced. I jettisoned my husband, the church, and God. I was very involved in the civil rights movement and found there a passion and a connection that I never had seen or felt in a church. In fact, I now held religion and the church largely responsible for the sins of humans in the manner in which we treated each other.

Despite radical changes in my life between the ages of thirty and fifty, nothing changed or matured in my sense of religion. I had opened my heart to others, to justice, to the thrill of standing for a principle. But religion mattered only in times of great stress, generally if I was afraid I was going to die, or afraid I had done something so terrible that there would be great consequences in the hereafter.

In my mid-fifties, the ground beneath me began shifting. There is something about turning fifty, I think, that triggers such activities of the soul. Parents and friends die, children leave home, worries begin about whether you are accomplishing whatever you are meant to accomplish in life. I finally began asking the questions I never had asked: What exists beyond what I see, hear, smell, and touch? Why should I behave morally? Why should I care about anyone else? Is there a duty to serve others? Can I be at peace? Can I wake up in the morning and face the day with joy?

I began reading, talking, and (oh gosh what a change) reflecting. I had read everything about mainline Christianity that I ever wanted to read, so I read things that were new to me, like Deepak Chopra, Marianne Williamson, Neale Donald Walsch, and Thomas Moore.

I became interested in Eastern ideas of meditation, reflection, and silence. I went to an ashram for a weekend. It was wonderful. It was like coming home. I found in these many experiences of exploring inward through workshops, meditation retreats, reading, and praying that followed, an inner resource I had never known existed.

When my mind is still, when I am silent, God can come in. God may be god. God may be goddess. God may be spirit. God may be the universe. I don't know, and I don't care. I really have no interest in theory.

My experience of myself became one of being a small part of a perfect whole. My experience is that I am as much a part of the whole as I am its co-creator. My life is my creation. I am responsible for every aspect of it. I need no material resources for being at peace and experiencing joy. I am supported by the rest of the whole in living my life, thus there is no need to worry. When I pray, I pray to my ancestors, to Ditri, the angel who came to me in a dream, to Sita, the Hindu Goddess, and to my friend Leigh who died at age fifty-five. I pray for wisdom, for love, for acceptance of whatever is. I forgive myself for the judgment machine that I am, and I ask for blessings on all other parts of God's creation.

Is it religion? Probably not. It is, however, a spiritual blessing to me. I now have the depth, the resources, and the peace to be of use to myself and the world. It is more than enough.

YOUR TURN
Discussion Questions:
1. What is faith? What is spirituality?
2. How has the way you were raised affected your current faith/spirituality?
3. Is it possible to have spirituality without faith? Is it possible to have faith without spirituality? Why or why not?
4. Do you think faith and spirituality deepen as we age? If so, how?

Individual Exercise: *What You Believe*

If you haven't given serious thought to what it is you believe in—your strength, your bedrock—it may be time to do so.
1. Write, in seven sentences, a statement of your beliefs. Take as much time as you want to craft the seven sentences. **Don't read further until you have completed this part of the exercise.**
2. Now turn to a clean page in your notebook. Again in seven sentences, describe what you believed in when you were a child. **Don't read further until you have completed this part of the exercise.**
3. Finally, turn to a new clean page. Again describe your beliefs in seven sentences. This time, however, write with your *non-dominant hand*, and write as quickly as possible. Do not stop to think. Just write seven sentences. **Don't read on until you have completed this part of the exercise.**
4. When you are finished, compare the three written pieces. How are they alike? How are they different? How different are your adult beliefs from your childhood beliefs? Did anything surprise you in what you wrote with your non-dominant hand? Are you content with your beliefs as they now are?

Group Exercise: *Discover the Unifying Principle*
1. Divide yourselves into groups by the belief system you now have.
2. Stand in different parts of the room based on your belief system: *e.g.,* Catholic, Protestant, Jewish, Muslim, spiritual, agnostic, atheist.
3. Look around the room and appreciate the different belief systems represented.

4. Come back together and discuss:
    *   Do the differences in beliefs affect the relationships of people in the room?
    *   Is there one principle from all of the beliefs and religions that is true for all participants?

Assignment:

Pretend you are the fourth author of *Saving the Best for Last* and write your story about "Faith and Spirituality" in your notebook.

Our Mothers

Her face is usually the first we recognize. Her voice the first we respond to. Her scent the first we turn toward. And in most cases, some variation of "mommy" is the first word we utter. She will continue to define our world, for better or for worse, for decades to come.

Most of us loved our mothers unconditionally until the maturational process simultaneously produced both pimples and a sudden recognition that our mothers were seriously flawed. Somewhere along the years, we softened. Perhaps our mothers weren't quite as ignorant as we had believed. Perhaps they knew what to say when our hearts were first broken or our first children were born. Whenever that moment occurred, it changed our relationship with our mothers yet again. For others of us, our mothers' lives became examples of what we didn't want for ours. We accepted that while they made certain choices we didn't agree with, we would make other choices for our own lives.

We have passed through the stages of blind adoration and frustration and dismissal. Many of us have, ourselves, become mothers of daughters. We have come out on the other side of the mother-daughter relationship. We have achieved the age that allows us to know our mothers for the first time. The knowledge gained fills us with joy, with pain, with anger, and ultimately with hard-won understanding. Whether we consciously strive to be like them, or to be as unlike them as possible, the fact remains that we are our mothers' daughters. These are the women who shaped us, and in so doing, affected the way we shape our lives and our own daughters.

At the time we started writing this book, we three were in very different situations mother-wise. Renee had lost her mother relatively early in life and had experienced most of her adult life without her. She was now at the age her own mother was when she died. Joyce's mother had a recurrence of breast cancer and died while we were writing the book. Jean's mother, while still living and in good physical health, was just beginning to experience the first stages of Alzheimer's. Each of us was in a state of mourning: Renee for the mother she never knew as an adult, Joyce for the mother who had just passed, and Jean for the mother who was "leaving" while still here.

This was, for many reasons, a very difficult chapter to write but one that was of utmost importance. Like many women, none of us had yet fully explored our relationships with our mothers. But loss impelled us to put pen to paper and, to varying degrees, express the hitherto unsaid. Each of us hit walls at times. We stalled, we wavered, we cried when we read our words to each other. And when we chose to write what should have been, rather than what was, we forced each other to get real, to go back, and to write again. The results were of greater value than we could have imagined.

RENEE

When my mother was five years younger than I am now, she began to feel the effects of lymphosarcoma, a fatal form of lymphatic cancer. She was diagnosed five years later, and two days after that, she died. I was twenty-four years old when my mother became ill. Over the next five years, I watched her fade, until, diagnosis or not, it was obvious that she was dying.

Through it all, my mother acted as though the increasing pain and debilitation of her life was no more significant than a case of the flu. She refused to talk about her illness, and so no one else spoke about it either.

At the time of her death, I believed that it wasn't until she contracted cancer that she chose to hold herself back from the people who loved her. I believed she either denied reality, or that she chose to protect us from the reality she recognized. What I didn't know at the time of her death was that my mother's secrets started with her birth and not merely with her illness. She loved me, she protected me, and she dispensed wise advice. And through it all, she never revealed anything of herself to me. I found out after she died that I didn't know anything about her at all.

My mother gave me the greatest gift a parent can give a child: total, unconditional love. There was never anything I could do to make her disappointed in me or angry with me. She cried once because of something I did. Her tears hit me harder than a slap in the face. But, in her desire to protect me from the traumas of her own life, she denied me the gift of intimacy.

She knew me and she understood me, but she didn't allow me to know or to understand *her*. My mother never talked about the circumstances of her birth or of her childhood. Most of what I know about her life was told to me by people after her death. I don't even know if all of the information is true. Some was told to me by my mother's uncle, then in his late eighties and becoming increasingly forgetful. My mother's half sister, a woman who has battled emotional demons for most of her life, told me the rest.

The bits and pieces of my mother's life are like shards of pottery. I can piece them together, but I can't be certain if the reconstruction is true to what was originally there. She was born in Russia and her mother died giving birth to her. Her father abandoned her, came to the Unites States, and remarried. Some years later, his second wife found out about the baby he left behind and convinced him to bring her here. By then, he had two more children and wasn't interested in an immigrant child. Eventually, though, he sent for her.

My mother was illegally placed on a ship and brought to the United States, an eight year-old thrown onto the doorstep of a father who didn't want her and into a world she didn't understand. My grandfather made fun of her and wouldn't help her to assimilate. My grandfather was a master at verbally abusing and degrading his wife and children. My step-grandmother did the best she could to care for my mother, but my step-grandmother was ultimately under my grandfather's control. She remained illiterate in the English language because he didn't allow her to attend night classes.

My grandfather pulled my mother out of school at age sixteen, sent her to work in a factory, and then made fun of her because she was a stupid, unskilled laborer. On weekends, she was given a pushcart filled with vegetables and pulled it several miles to join the other vendors along South Street in Philadelphia. Throughout the winter, no matter what the weather, she went to the market and stood there all day until her goods were sold. My mother wanted more for her life. She went to school at night and got her high school diploma. Then she attended a business school at night and graduated. She left the factory and got a job as a keypunch operator at the Federal Reserve Bank. She continued to live at home, and she gave most of her paycheck to my grandfather.

Eventually, she fell in love with a good, decent man who wanted to marry her. But she was of greater value to my grandfather unmarried, and so he forbade her to marry. She broke up with her suitor. Some years later, my mother's half sister wanted to marry. Jewish tradition dictated that a younger sister couldn't marry until the older sister was married. For this reason, my grandfather told my mother to find a husband immediately. Again, she complied. Someone fixed her up with my father, and she quickly married him. She was thirty-three years old. She did as my grandfather instructed.

My father was born in Poland. Like my mother, he came to this country illegally. He was quiet and soft spoken. He must have seemed a welcome relief at first to the loud, in-your-face, abusive kind of control that my grandfather favored. But my father had his own non-negotiable demands. My mother was told to give up all of her friends and her outside interests. My father believed that friends and outside interests were permissible until one married. After that, a person should only associate with family. In all the years I was growing up, I remember only one occasion in which a non-family member came to our house.

I spent the first seven years of my life living a few houses away from my grandparents. My grandparents lived on the first floor of a duplex. My uncle lived with them, and my aunt and her husband lived on the floor above them. My grandfather continued to exercise his control over all of us whenever he could. After my parents and I moved to another neighborhood, he would call my mother every day and keep her on the phone for what seemed like hours, yelling at her, and complaining about everyone and everything in his life. She would sit and repeat, "Yes, Pop" over and over until he would release her.

I will always feel that my own selfish view of life prevented me from seeing the pain under my mother's smile. I chose to believe her when she said that she loved my father, that she had everything she ever wanted in life, and that she never had other children because I was so perfect. I chose to believe it all in spite of what I saw in reality. I chose to believe it because to have questioned her ran the risk of her telling me the truth and that would have placed a responsibility on me that I didn't want. I was not prepared to mother my mother.

And, although I saw the dynamics between my grandfather and the rest of the family and heard the shouting, I blocked it out. My grandfather exempted me from his wrath. I was his only grandchild, and I could do no wrong. He was loving and affectionate toward me. It was easier to choose that reality of my grandfather over the one I saw destroying everyone else around him. It was only when I made the decision to marry a non-Jew that I saw a small part of my grandfather's damaging behavior. It was enough.

Contrary to what my mother always told me, she later admitted that I was an only child because after my birth, my grandfather came to the house each day and stayed all day. Both she and my father believed that he intended to take my affection away from my father and give it to him. My father threatened to leave my mother unless she stopped my grandfather from coming over. My mother did, but the emotional toll was too great on her. She chose not to have any more children.

My mother and I once visited cousins in New York, cousins no one else in the family ever spoke of. I saw photos of my mother posing with people I couldn't identify at the 1939 New York Worlds Fair. My grandparents, aunt, and uncle weren't in any of the photos. She told me that these people were her family, but they never seemed to be connected to the family I knew. If they were her family, who was she? Where did she belong? Where did *I* belong? I found out many years later that my birth grandmother's family was all in New York. They wanted a relationship with my mother, and she wanted one with them. My grandfather wanted no contact with them whatsoever and so any contact my mother was able to have with them came in later years when she was older and more independent.

My mother was an amazing cook. One of the best things that ever happened to her was that a few people found out about her gift and persuaded her to sell them pastries for special occasions. The word spread, and soon people started calling the house on a regular basis. There were so many calls, in fact, that my mother started a small catering operation from our basement. I think my father went along with it because the business crept up on them and because she didn't have to work out of the house. His only demand was that it be a *kosher* catering operation.

After a few years, the revenue from the catering allowed my parents to take a real vacation for the first time ever and to go on their first cruise. They began to put money into a savings account. For the first time, my mother was in control of her life. Several years later, she became ill.

I'm angry with my mother, angry that she allowed everyone else to be more important than she was, angry that she denied my knowing her, angry that she never left her father's control and had the life she wanted. I am angriest with me for not allowing myself to see the pain she lived with. I blinded myself to her pain because I didn't want it in my own life. My questions to her about her life were always tentative, and her answers were always positive. I accepted what she said because to have done otherwise would have placed a burden on me.

My mother is an enigma to me. She is at once stronger than I could ever be and weaker than I would ever allow myself to be. She permitted my grandfather to convince her that she was worthless, but in so doing, she became the validation for the worth of everyone around her. She was the ear everyone poured their troubles into. She was the hand everyone needed to hold. She was the shoulder to cry on and the arms that held her dying stepmother.

I used to believe that my greatest wish would be to be able to sit on her lap again with her arms around me and share my pain with her. I would have had her turn my confusion into conviction, to have seen me through my separation and the crazy years that followed, to have told me that my choices didn't ruin my children's lives.

I believed that my greatest wish would be to have shared my joy with her, to have had her know my children as they grew into adulthood, to have seen the powerful independent life I have created for myself, to have read my novel and short stories, to have seen my love song to her woven through the pages.

I still want all that. But now there is something I want more. I am now the age my mother was when she died. I see the world in a different way than I did in my childhood, and I see my mother in a different way. I am no longer merely her daughter. Because death fixed her age at the age I am now, I feel at once both her daughter and her contemporary.

I want to be able to talk to her as an equal, two women of a certain age who have come from different circumstances and have each made different choices in life. I want her to tell me her story, and I want to tell her mine. I want to know the child she was and the woman she became. I want to tell her that I have never held anything back from my

own daughter, that I have chosen to tell my daughter about the damaging choices I made in my life, and that my daughter still sees me as her role model and best friend.

I want to tell my mother that the worst she has to tell me about her life wouldn't change my love or respect for her, that she will always be my ideal of what it means to have courage and compassion and to give unconditional love.

I want her to forgive me for not having seen her emotional pain, for not having pushed her to reveal, for not having provided her the comfort that had always been denied her. I want her to forgive me for capitulating to the doctors' wishes, in the final hours of her life, when she contracted encephalitis. They convinced me to authorize a spinal tap, and I did, knowing that she was dying anyway. While the procedure was carried out, I stood on the other side of the hospital room door and listened to her tortured moans. I was filled with a feeling of terrible power that haunts me still.

I want her to forgive me.

I will never be able to accomplish any of this. My mother's life can now only be lived in my memory and in the characteristics I see developing daily in my children. In one or another of them, I see a generosity of spirit, gentleness, compassion and humanity. It is these, out of all my mother's traits, I hold most closely and value most highly in my children. As my children continue to create their adult lives, I will call upon these traits myself as I continue to parent them. I know my mother would have done no less.

JOYCE

My mother, Anna May, died one year ago. I still have not yet recovered my balance. I am suspended in space, floating, drifting. I hold my breath. I wait. I want the pain gone. I want to experience the joy of her again.

I long to touch her, to have her touch me, to feel her arms around me, to see her face light up at the sight of me, and to hear her sweet voice. I yearn to smell her. I long to be with her, to hold her hand, to play and dance as we always did. Sometimes I fear I will lose my memory of her. The voices in my head say that she is in a better place and that she no longer feels any pain . Her spirit is free.

I loved her dearly, and she knew it. The last words I said to her before she lost consciousness in the hospital emergency room were, "I love you, Mom." She squeezed my hand because she could no longer talk.

I am the oldest of seven children. My mother knew beyond a doubt that all of her children, their spouses and partners, their children, and her great-grandchildren, adored her. As the matriarch of our huge family, Mom reveled in being the center of attention. My mother was an only child and told me many times about how she had always wanted seven children. I don't know if that was true or not, but she gave birth to the seven of us and made it clear that she chose us. In all of my life, my mother never ever said anything that would have had us believe otherwise.

It took me many years to see what a powerful, strong, loving woman she was, and how blessed I was to have her as my mother. As I was growing up, I felt otherwise. I despised her weakness, the kind of weakness that would allow her to tolerate my father's violence that was so damaging to all of us. I could not understand her, and I vowed to myself that I would never be like my mother.

Looking back, I know I fell into the same trap with my father as my mother did. My father sexually abused me from the time I was too young to remember until I was sixteen years old. I allowed him to abuse me because he told me that if I reported him, he would go to jail, and we children would be sent off to an orphanage never to see each other again. For many years, I believed him.

I know my mother believed she was doing the best that she could by staying with my father. She had seven young kids and no way to support them. When I finally did decide to stand up for myself and tell my mother of my father's abuse, my mother tried to throw my father out. He was not going to leave. He threatened to get a gun and kill us all. While they argued, I went next door and called the police. My mother told the police the truth when they came to our door, and they arrested my father and drove him off to jail. It was the first time I experienced my mother standing up for me. She believed what I had told her. She chose me over my father.

The impact of all of these events on my mother was devastating. She began to unravel before my eyes. Mom no longer cooked, did nothing to keep the house, and acted more like a teenager than I did. With my father in jail, my mother seemed unable to function. She began frequenting bars nearly every night with her cousin, often staying out until dawn. She began drinking for the first time in her life. One morning, she brought home a man she had just met whom she claimed was going to take her and all of us kids off to Texas to live. I thought she had lost her mind. I was furious with her for believing the stranger and for leaving me with the responsibility of taking care of my brothers and sisters.

Our roles reversed. I became the mother. I took care of my brothers and sisters and saw that they got fed. I was the one waiting on the front stoop for her, demanding to know where she had been all night. My mother became my daughter. How dare she leave us alone? How dare she frighten and worry me? Just when our lives were freed up from the tyranny of my father, my mother abandoned us emotionally.

I believe all of this happened because she could not handle the knowledge of what I had endured. All those years that she convinced herself she was doing what was best for her children, my father was molesting me. Now he was going to the penitentiary while we were trying to survive on welfare. I was sixteen, and the youngest of the seven of us was six. My mother's world was blown apart when all the deceptions and lies of more than a decade came to light.

After months of waiting, my father's trial took place, and he began a ten-year sentence. Mom began to recover from the shock of my revelation and the trial. She began to adjust to life without my father. She again took on her role as mother. She tried to re-establish a connection with me.

I was angry, and I would not accept her coming back into my life as an authority figure and a support. As much as I did not want the responsibility of caring for my family and being the decision-maker, I did not want to give up my control. I thought I was smarter, stronger, and more decisive than my mother. I could do anything better than she could. I did not need her to mother me, and I did not trust her. It was okay for everyone in the family to need me. That was more comfortable for me than my needing them.

I did not want to hear anything my mother had to say to me. At one point when I was eighteen I had a confrontation with her that I have never forgotten. She shook her fist at me when I frustrated her and made her angry. She told me, "You're going to find out that you need people, that you can't do everything yourself!"

Years later, when I was in my thirties, the breakup of my marriage was my ticket to therapy. For the first time in my life, I began to deal with the incest and my subsequent trust issues. I could no longer deny that I would not allow anyone to get close to me. I acknowledged that I maintained barriers that made intimacy impossible. At the same time, I prided myself on my strength, my success at holding myself together, and my ability to discuss my past with great ease. I was incapable of crying; I learned when I was younger to steel myself and never to show my pain to my father and others.

In therapy, I discovered more than I ever expected to face. I was very aware of how my father had hurt me. I had lived my life being his victim and being angry. I hated him. That was the easy part. On the other hand, I had never thought about my mother's role in the abuse. I never wanted to believe that my mother might have known what was happening when my father was abusing me. Yet in therapy, I came to recognize that it was a possibility. I turned the anger I had always directed at my father on my mother.

This period was one of the hardest of my life. I did not want to face knowing my mother may have known at some level what was happening to me and had not protected me. I felt completely betrayed and devastated. I did not want to let in the pain of this discovery.

I spent many sessions with my therapist weighing the pros and cons of discussing this with my mother. I saw that I had a choice. I had to decide what it would cost both of us if I confronted her.

I chose not to do so. I simply made a decision, with the support of my therapist, to forgive my mother without knowing whether my mother knew or not. I chose to believe that she would have acted on my behalf if she had known. I will never know if that is true. In retrospect, I most likely chose to forgive her because I did not want to know the truth. In my final analysis, I decided that having a relationship with my mother was more important than making her wrong. If having a relationship with her was what I wanted most, then nothing else mattered. I put the past behind me and never looked back.

My choice to forgive my mother was the best decision I could have made, and I have never regretted it. I never told her about my process and that I had forgiven her. I felt we both had been through enough. I put my grief and anger about her behind me, and in my mid-thirties, I created a loving, connected relationship with her. I began to see her with new eyes, and as the decades rolled on, I discovered how lucky I was to be her daughter.

Mom and I did have some discussions about what happened and how she felt about it. She voiced her sorrow for all I had endured and told me she felt helpless with seven children and was afraid she couldn't support us if she left my father. She asked for my forgiveness.

Then as I was turning forty, I had a dinner with my sisters and Mom to tell them about an interview I gave to a reporter for a new women's magazine. When I told my sisters that I was going public with my story, they reacted loudly with differing opinions about the sense or insanity of my revelations. As they argued the pros and cons, my mother, sitting beside me, leaned over, and said in my ear, "You know, I must have known." It was the first time she admitted that to me. I was stunned. I did not reply. I just took it in.

Later when I reflected on what she said, I began to have a real sense of how strong and courageous she was. I thought she was a hell of a woman to say that to me. I was still struggling with how to put the past behind me and heal myself, and it would take more years of work before I felt free of the burden of victimhood, but I experienced relief and gratitude for what my mother said to me. I was touched by her vulnerability.

When my mother's breast cancer metastasized to her lungs two years ago, I experienced a sense of suspended animation. After my initial shudder of fear in the doctor's office, I braced myself. I held my breath. I tried not to feel anything. My mother's doctor said, "You do understand what I am saying, don't you? You have cancer again." It was like he was saying it to me. My mother nodded her head while I sat there knowing that this was a battle my eighty-one year-old mother might not win. She took it on as she did everything in life, without bitterness or complaint, trusting the doctors and God to make her well. As usual, she seemed to roll with the punches, adjusting to what life dished up, and made it clear that whatever God had in store for her, she trusted that she could handle it.

I knew the implications. Almost everything I read as I searched the Internet said that if we were lucky, Mom might have a year. I never shared this fact with my brothers and sisters. I didn't want them to treat her like she was dying. I wanted us all to enjoy every moment she was alive, to be present in the moment. I tried to prepare myself for what might come, but I could not do it. I could not imagine life without her.

As she suffered unspeakable pain, she still managed to keep up a brave front. When she was able to talk and sit up in her bed, she proudly told all of us kids that the hospital staff voted her "best patient."

My prayers for her were that she would not suffer more pain and that if she survived the surgery and treatment, her quality of life would allow her to continue as she had been doing when her cancer was in remission. Her greatest joy was hanging out with all of us and being on the go.

She surprised all seven of us that Christmas with a check. She gave us $2,000 apiece, practically all she had left of her savings. I can still see her face, the shining delight in her smile that was a reflection of my surprise at the gift. She said, "I want to see you enjoy this while I'm alive." She made each of us tell her how we would use the money. She loved to see us happy. I believe she knew that she didn't have much longer with us.

She died two months later.

I know my life will never be the same. When all of the family gets together, it is not the same. No one can replace her. We all looked forward to being with her. She was the center of our universe.

I have chosen to be the matriarch of my family. I told my brothers and sisters that we take up where Mom left off. She didn't want to see any of us fall through the cracks. None of my siblings questions our mission to take care of and love one another. That's what Mom wanted.

In my youth, my mother was not the mother I wanted. I rejected her, loathed her seeming weaknesses and her dysfunctional relationship with my father. I could not see anything about her to respect. Years later, after I made the decision to forgive her, I was able to create a love and respect that opened up many other possibilities for my life, including my close ties with my brothers and sisters and their spouses.

Choosing to forgive her opened the way for me to forgive my father years later. Today I believe that to forgive is the most powerful way to live. I would not have it any other way. [*Author's Note: I wrote this a year after my mother died on February 24, 2003.*]

JEAN

My mother is from a family of Welsh coal miners who didn't display affection or discuss feelings. She, like me, has been for most of her life intent on controlling her environment and everyone in it. She, like me, is very strong-willed. I saw her as critical and judgmental, never giving praise or approval. I did not see myself as critical or judgmental.

My mother would say things like, "Do you really like your hair that way?" or "Why did you get a "B" (in the midst of all "A's") in Science?" I saw each statement as criticism and attack. I was doing everything I knew how to do to make her proud of me, yet it seemed that criticism was what was returned. It was so important to have my mother's respect that it was the subject of my bedtime prayers well into high school. "Now I lay me down to sleep...and please never let me do anything that would shame my mother or father. Please make my mother proud of me." That was my litany.

On the surface all was well in our relationship. I loved my mother and merely designated her as a person who was difficult to please.

Under the surface, I was conflicted and miserable and at a loss as to how to gain my mother's respect.

When I married and had children, I believed I was on the track to making my mother proud, since she placed a high value on marriage and children. It didn't work. Criticism continued. "Is that all your children eat for breakfast?" "Don't you think you are harming your children by working?"

I remember once sitting in a room full of relatives, talking about a cousin's teenage child. "Are you going to let her go *away* to college?" asked my mother. "Yes," said my cousin. "Oh," offered my mother, disapproval and/or disappointment in her tone. "Why do you say that?" asked the cousin. I too waited, with no clue as to what my mother's answer would be. "Well," she said, "I think that was where we went wrong with Jean."

My reaction to my mother's criticisms would sometimes result in my cutting off communication for long periods of time. Once we didn't speak for many months because my mother (a "you-can-eat-off-the floor" housekeeper) gave me advance notice that on my young family's next visit, she would like us to be neater. I immediately cancelled the visit. Excoriating my mother for her choice of form over content, I wrote her a letter explaining that I, unlike her, ran a home in which people felt welcome at all times. I railed that I chose people over things. Another time, much later when my daughters were grown, my mother expressed her disapproval and dislike of the man I was living with. It wasn't the fact that we were living together without benefit of matrimony, although goodness knows she didn't like that either; she thought he was rude and hostile to her and a terrible influence on me. That time I didn't speak to her for almost a year.

My reaction cured nothing. I was miserable getting criticism, and I was miserable being on the outs with my mother. While I was aware enough to know that the purpose of my attacks on my mother was to establish how different from her (and superior to her) I was, the half of me that intensely wanted my mother's respect was fully feeling my failure to get it. I had not lived up to my mother's standards. No matter how much I yelled, all I really wanted was for my mother to say, "I'm so proud of you."

And so we stumbled on for years, from my perspective always

setting conditions that limited the quality of the relationship. I thought the problem was very simple: if my mother would stop criticizing, if she would just acknowledge all the good things I've done in my life, she and I would have no problems. It did not occur to me that I, by myself, could heal the wounds; that I, by myself, could create exactly the loving relationship I craved.

There are two factors that made it possible for me to change the relationship I had with my mother. First, I have been on the receiving end of my own daughters' reactions to me, and, through them, gained perspective on my relationship with my mother. I got to see how my daughters' values were shaped in large part by their judgments of me and how I lived my life. For example, they both now tell me that their dedication to staying in their marriages through some extremely rocky times is in direct reaction to my breaking up my marriage when they were eight and ten years old. They did not like that I asked for a divorce, and they did not like me for doing it. They took the divorce personally and made later life decisions based on this hurt.

It was only when I had a life experience of mother/daughter cause and effect that I began to step back and see I had always taken personally my mother's actions and reactions. As a daughter, I believed that my mother's actions or reactions were personal to me. In fact, it seems they usually had nothing whatsoever to do with me. They had to do with her.

Second, and most importantly, I got to see how much like my mother I am. She was critical? Hah! I was critical of everything she said. She didn't tell me how proud she was of me? My mother went to nursing school when I was in high school. She went to school full-time, kept the house in its usual perfect condition, and had breakfast and dinner on the table every day for my father, sisters, and me. She had very little, if any, help or encouragement from me and very little recognition for her accomplishments. There was some notion in my mind that if you tell people how wonderful they or their accomplishments are, they might get a "swelled head." It never occurred to me that my mother's withholding acknowledgement of my accomplishments came from the same root.

I saw how much I longed for her respect and how little I gave to her. I knew how her criticism hurt me, and finally saw how my lack of respect must hurt her. Once I saw that, it was a short step to seeing my mother through entirely new eyes. I had criticized my mother for years, yet I knew that underneath all that criticism I loved her. What if the same was true for her? What if criticism was her way of expressing care and love?

A new world opened. When I heard everything she said as loving, it was loving. When I raised no defense to criticism, it not only stopped, it turned to praise. When I gave respect and acknowledgement, I received the same from my mother. When I softened, she softened. Oh my goodness, what a miracle.

For the next several years my mother and I loved to be together. We lived a thousand miles apart, but talked at least weekly on the phone, usually more often. I visited a minimum of every three months. My mother and I hugged and gossiped. We got up early, took our arthritis pills, and talked about family secrets. We poked fun at each other's foibles, and we always shared our passion for dance: how it made us feel to be out there on the floor moving to the music.

This was a golden period that I wanted to go on and on and on, even though I knew that could not be. I finally had my mother the way we dream of having our mothers. Yet, in the midst of it, she was saying good-bye. Her memory and ability to hold anything in it faded rapidly and frighteningly. She no longer remembered things that were important to her, no less things that were important to me.

Then the worst happened. My father died. My father, my mother's life companion. My parents had always said they would leave together, but my father couldn't wait.

My mother deteriorated rapidly without my father. Every visit I saw that her memory loss reached further and further back in time. On my last visit, she didn't know me immediately. I caught the confusion in her eyes – just for a minute. Then she asked, "Are you really here, or am I dreaming?"

My mother died the Friday before Mother's Day, almost a year to the day from my father's death. I am in mourning for my father and my mother. I know, though, that I am a blessed daughter. The absolute gift I was given over the last years was the gift of basking in my mother's love. I treasured and still treasure every moment I had with her. And now I have a new purpose: to pass on this love, this accepting, respecting love, to my daughters and to my daughters' daughters. What a wonderful gift to have and share.

YOUR TURN
Discussion Questions:
1. Why do you think the mother/daughter relationship is so significant?
2. If you had a good relationship with your mother, what made it a good relationship?
3. If your relationship with your mother was difficult, why? Do you think it is possible to change the relationship you have with your mother? What if she is no longer here?

Individual Exercises:
Exercise One: *Speaking To Mother*
1. Write a letter to your mother. It doesn't matter whether you ever knew your mother. It doesn't matter whether your mother is living or dead. It doesn't matter whether you and your mother had a good relationship.
2. In your letter, thank your mother for three things. It doesn't matter if these are big or small things as long as they are real to you. Even if you don't think your mother was a very good mother, find three things for which to thank her.
3. When the letter is complete, read it to your mother. If she is alive, read it to her in person or over the phone if that is the only possibility. If your mother is no longer living, read the letter out loud to her, and know she hears it.

Exercise Two: *Speaking As Mother*
1. Sit alone in a quiet place, preferably somewhere in nature. Go back in time to when you were a child, back to the first clear memory you have of your mother. Think about what she looked like, how she sounded, what she smelled like.
2. When you can see your mother in your mind's eye, take the part of your mother. Become your mother. Speak as your mother. Talk out loud. Explain, as your mother, what her life was like when you were a child. Don't think about what you are going to say as your mother. Just open your mouth and let the words come out. If you have any specific "why" questions you would like to ask your mother, do so. Then answer as your mother. Just let it flow.
3. When you are finished, when there is no more to say,

nothing more to ask, close your eyes and be still for at least three minutes. Just let your emotions settle. Then get out your notebook and record what you believe you learned from this exercise.

Group Exercise: *Hearing With New Ears*

We all have practiced in our minds, repeatedly, the "stories" of what happened to us. When such a story is told aloud, repeatedly, and from different perspectives, it lessens the dramatic impact on us.

You will need a timekeeper for this exercise.

1. Get into pairs. Sit directly facing each other—knee to knee. Pick a Partner A and a Partner B. Partner A will speak for one minute relating one specific incident from her childhood with her mother that illustrates what negative things her mother "did" to her. Example: I came downstairs, dressed for my prom and my mother said, *"Do you really want to wear your hair like that?"* I was so hurt it ruined my evening. Explain the circumstances and how it made you feel. Partner B's job is to pay full attention to what is being said.

2. Partner A will speak again for one minute, but this time she will relate only the facts of the same incident—no conclusions, emotions or judgments. Example: I came downstairs dressed for my prom. My mother said to me *"Do you really want to wear your hair like that?"* I went to the prom.

3. Partner A will speak again for one minute. This time she will tell the story as though it was the best thing that ever happened to her. It should be told with energy and enthusiasm. Example: Just before I was to leave for the prom, my mother said to me, *"Do you really want to wear your hair like that?"* I was SO grateful that she noticed that my hairstyle really didn't complement my dress!

4. Partner B will then repeat the steps as Partner A listens.

5. The group will join together and discuss what it felt like to tell the story in three ways.
   - Was it difficult to tell your story in different ways? Did you find you were very wed to your original interpretation of events?
   - Did you have a different experience when telling your

story in different ways?

- Do you see how the manner in which you tell a story can reinforce interpretations of events, interpretations that you made up as a child?
- Can you see that retelling the story sometimes allows you to have a new view of long ago events and may free you to see yourself and others in new ways?

Assignment:

Pretend you are the fourth author of *Saving the Best for Last* and write your story about "My Mother" in your notebook.

Loss

The inevitable consequence of aging is that our losses multiply. Death is the loss many of us will think of first. Most of the people who defined our world in childhood will eventually leave it. Many of the friends we have accumulated along the way will be lost. Some losses, like divorce, may seem as painful as a death, but unlike death, will have no finality.

Other losses will simply mark the passage of time. Our innocence may be lost early or late, but eventually it will go. Body parts may seem to relocate to other areas of our bodies or be snatched entirely from us. Our memories may become as elusive as our car keys. The loss of our eyesight, our hearing, our teeth, our hair, will have us believing at times that we ourselves are disappearing in increments. Our sense of balance, given a temporary reprieve by sensible shoes, will eventually fail. Some of us will lose our minds, but others will blame that on motherhood.

The fact is, the longer we live, the more losses we will sustain. We can complain, we can grieve, we can mourn, we can avoid. We will sustain loss nonetheless. We three have experienced devastating loss in many of its forms. We have each suffered, and we have each found something unexpected in the process.

RENEE

The losses in my life began to occur well before I was born. Family members disappeared in the Holocaust, taking their histories and their futures with them. And, as though only their presence gave solidity to the places they inhabited, the towns disappeared as well.

Whims of fate swallowed up others: In the years following World

169

War I, in an era that had few automobiles and little traffic, a car found my uncle as he was crossing the street. One grandmother died during childbirth, another from unknown causes. Depending on my father's mood during the telling, my grandfather died of either a broken heart or a damaged one. All that was left of one cousin was a small unframed photo of a toddler seated in a wicker chair. Large dark eyes stare out at the camera lens. A name which I cannot read is inscribed on the back. "It is the only photo ever taken of her. She died young," the only explanation.

As the only child of my parents and the only grandchild of my grandparents, each loss had already narrowed the world into which I was born. Families have been described as tapestries. Mine was more like a piece of crochet. I knew that the threads somehow held the piece together, but my family's threads always seemed too fragile, too tenuous. When I tried to follow the threads, as careful as I might have been, I always ended up in the spaces in between.

Because my mother was ashamed of the circumstances of her birth and that she was an immigrant, she never spoke of her birth mother's family or of her life in Russia. My grandfather's brother once mentioned the name of a town, half-remembered across too many decades and too many miles.

Before I was out of my twenties, my mother died. This loss, unlike the others, would be a very different kind of experience for me. Unlike the other family members who had passed, I was there to witness my mother's passing in its most minute increments. My mother's death was slow, and her life wound down over a period of five or six years. Her disease was, for most of those years, unnamed and untreated. I lived with a strange mixture of rage and love, wanting a diagnosis and not wanting it.

Her death made no sense to me, and I wasn't prepared to accept it. It felt more like, if not a mistake, than a terrible omission of some sort. For weeks afterward, I racked my brain to remember what it was that I had forgotten. If I could only remember what it was (a thought, an action, a belief), I could bring her back. It is thirty years later, and part of me will always be in some kind of strange limbo, like a child still attached to the umbilical cord but floating outside her mother's body.

Before I turned fifty, both my father and my close friend Miki had died. I believe that my father's death actually occurred at the same time as my mother's. Before she was even in the ground, his bags were packed, and he was prepared to go. But for some reason, his luggage wasn't collected for another seventeen years. He wasn't sick. He simply got tired of waiting for death to notice him. He stopped eating, and he eventually got to where he wanted to go.

My friend Miki's death, like my mother's, had me feeling impotent and in a rage. Miki's death was one of medical oversight. Like my mother, she had too much to give to the world and too little time to do it.

I don't believe death, or the way we die, has anything at all to do with how well or how nobly we live our lives. Many good people die terrible deaths. Many good people die young. Many bad people live long and live well. And, unlike those who believe in the notions of heaven and hell, I don't believe in a direct eternal reward or punishment for our actions.

If I've learned anything at all about death, it would be that death, like life, presents us with choices. As part of humanity, I am responsible for all lives no less than I am responsible for my own. And, in my own way, I get to represent the people who have passed on. The best way I can overcome my grief is to incorporate in myself some of what they had been. And, if their deaths occurred before I was born, I get to imagine the best of what they could have been. It doesn't change my sense of profound loss for what was, for what could have been. But for me, it is the only belief that turns that loss into any kind of possibility.

JOYCE

The loss that had the most profound effect on my life went unnoticed, unrecognized for what it was until decades after it happened. I was a child when I lost my childhood.

The loss began gradually. It started when my next sister was born two years after me, followed in close succession by five more siblings. My mother needed help with all the babies, so I was the big sister who learned to cook and iron, baby-sit and bathe my younger brothers and sisters, and fill in whenever my mother was too sick to get out of bed. As a young child, I had little time for play.

My father reminded me constantly that I was the oldest, that I must set an example for the younger children, that I must lead the way. Responsibility was drilled into my head. There was no room for making mistakes or goofing off. I became a serious child who took seriously my father's admonitions and the responsibilities thrust upon me by an overwhelmed mother.

But the act that completely robbed me of my childhood happened when my father began to sexually molest me at an age too young for me to remember. Scarier than the abuse itself was the belief that I could destroy my family due to my father's threats that if I said anything, my family would be split up and sent to various orphanages. I silently bore the responsibility to keep us together until I was 16, all the while mothering my siblings.

That was it. My childhood was gone, never to be recovered. I was old before my time. Even though I looked like a child, I never knew what it was like to *be* a child. I did not know how to do childlike or childish things. I didn't know how to have fun, I lost my sense of humor—if I ever had one—and silently resented anyone who had what I missed. My grandmother, who dearly loved me, told me I acted like an old lady when I was a girl, but I never knew how to be any other way.

Turning my father in to the police did not produce the freedom I hoped for because my family experienced pain and humiliation, and I experienced tremendous guilt and depression for asserting my needs and standing up for myself. The pattern was set. I grew into a woman who could trust no one, believing that I could rely only on myself for whatever I needed. And I was filled with rage.

It was only as an adult in therapy that I recognized how much I had detached myself from the traumatic life I lived on a daily basis. I was in denial. When I was at school, my life at home was unreal to me. It was like I was another person. Whatever was happening wasn't happening to me. How could it be when I was an outstanding student and leader among my peers?

When I later read about multiple or split personalities of people who had been severely traumatized in childhood, I could identify with them. Multiple Personality Disorder—now referred to as Dissociative Identity Disorder—is often associated with child abuse. The personality "splits" when the human psyche can no longer cope with the pain of abuse. I did not have multiple personalities, though I felt like it at times, and the only way I could function or cope was to disconnect from reality. I was numb.

Through my therapy I was able to recall what had happened to me, sometimes through hypnosis, and fully experience my pain and anger. I was finally able to cry and grieve the loss of my childhood and innocence. Eventually I let go of my rage and forgave my father.

My friends have wondered how I could forgive him. It took years of therapeutic intervention to finally recognize how rage and resentment propelled me, how I blamed my father for everything that was "wrong" with me. I was unable to let go of what weighed me down, even though I longed to put my past behind me.

With guidance from my therapist, I looked at my abuse from my father's point of view. Through his eyes, I could see that he was a victim of his own father's abuse, that he didn't really set out from the beginning to hurt me, and that he was sorry for what he had done to me. I know it sounds crazy to those who have not reached this stage of recovery, but once I was able to do that, I was able to understand my father in a way I had never seen him. When I was able to see through new eyes and understand him as a human being, I gained an insight and compassion I had never had.

I remember the moment I said the words, "I forgive you," to my father in that long ago therapy session. Although he was deceased, I knew he heard my words. That I said the words was more important than whether he heard them. The words transformed me from being a victim to gaining the emotional freedom I longed for. The words and my choice to forgive made it possible for me to move forward to live my life fully and to come into my own as a woman responsible for the way she responds as an adult. My words of forgiveness allowed me to sever the strings attached to my father and his abuse.

The only lasting residual effect of the abuse is depression. I experienced mild forms in my teens with occasional shifts to more encompassing depressive episodes where I experienced panic attacks and great anguish over my suicidal thoughts, but I never told anyone about them.

Through the years since then, I've learned that if I don't take action—and that is one of the hardest things for me to do in the midst of a depression—I will slip deeper and deeper into what feels like a dark hole until I am unable to cope and cannot climb out of it. Then it takes intensive therapy and medication to pull out of it. I've had three experiences like that, two of which occurred in my fifties. Now I know the danger signs well enough that I can generally take steps to help myself before I am fully in its grip.

The challenge for me in recovery is to stay conscious of my feelings. Right now I am seeing a therapist every six weeks or so to keep myself on track for my vision for my life and to be accountable to someone for the goals I've set. I'm using my therapist more as a life coach, but our sessions are always a good way for me to check in with myself and pay attention to what is going on with me. I find the sessions to be an excellent tool to stay on track emotionally and to stay healthy.

I have spent my entire life working toward recovery, an on-going process that, thankfully, is no longer the primary focus of my life today. These days I am at peace with what happened to me. I no longer grieve for something I never had and can never recover. I no longer experience pain or a feeling of deprivation.

I am finished mourning for the loss of my childhood. I instead focus my life on living with meaning and purpose. My life is a testimony to my recovery.

JEAN

I did not lose anyone close to me until I was over fifty years old. Yes, I lost friends to geographical moves, and I lost mates to the dissolution of relationships, but I never lost anyone to death. That made me very fortunate. It also made me very ignorant about loss. I had been around others who lost mothers, brothers, friends, and even children. I tried not to be around them because I was inadequate to respond in any way that made sense. I was frightened that I would say something horribly inappropriate or insensitive. The experience of death and grief was not imaginable to me. If I thought about it at all, I thought it was something that must feel terrible for a while, but would lessen with time.

I also thought there was a hierarchy of grief. If one lost a grandmother, for instance, that was to be expected and not so very painful. The loss of a relative like an aunt or cousin also was fairly distant. Losing a parent would have been more painful on my scale; then in increasing pain order would be the loss of a sibling, then a mate, then a child. That was the worst I could imagine, the death of one's child. But I didn't really know how it would feel.

In 1990, my grandmother died. She was ninety years old and had been completely lost to Alzheimer's ten years earlier. She lived those ten years in a world of horror and unremitting mental suffering. She recognized no one. She believed in every moment that she was being attacked. She thought everyone meant to harm her. Her death truly was a blessing to her and, I thought, to my parents who visited her every day without fail. I was amazed to see how my mother grieved over her mother's death. I didn't understand it, and I had little empathy for it.

My friend Leigh died in 1993 at age fifty-four. Leigh was one of the special angels of the world. She was a dancer who, at age sixteen, was struck down by polio and was left a quadriplegic. She had the use of the lower half of one arm only. Despite the obvious obstacles, Leigh earned her college degree and then a master's degree on a Woodrow Wilson Fellowship. She went into civil rights work, where I met her.

After twenty years, Leigh moved from Washington, D.C., where we worked together, to an island off the coast of Maine. She lived alone, with an aide to help her get up in the morning and go to bed at night. She took the ferry every day to her job, protecting the civil rights of kids in the public schools in Maine.

Leigh was a published poet and was partly through writing her autobiography when disaster struck. She called me one slow summer afternoon and said, "Can you come here? I have stomach cancer." I was shocked. How could this be? How could life be that unfair? How could Leigh have come through all she came through only to get stomach cancer? I went immediately to Maine and sat with her while she cried. At the same time she was crying, though, she also was planning the future.

She was creating a seminar on teen suicide for the State Education Agency, and she was ordering tickets for the Etta James concert.

Two weeks later her sister called me. Leigh was in a coma and not expected to live. I flew back to Maine. I didn't want to. I wanted to be on the way to anywhere but Leigh's bedside. I was so inadequate to go there. I had nothing wise to say. I didn't know how to be. But I went. Leigh was in a coma. She never regained consciousness. She died that day.

I didn't understand it. I didn't understand how she could be gone and why she would be gone. People were crying and in pain all around me. I couldn't wait to get away. Leigh was my friend, but I couldn't admit to the pain of her loss. I hurried back to D.C. and back to work. I didn't suffer from Leigh's loss, I just didn't think about it. I went on in this way, not feeling the pain that most people felt, not admitting loss into my world.

Then my sister Lynn's breast cancer metastasized and this shock blew up my world. Lynn was a pain-in-the-ass little sister. She was seven years younger than I. She was a drama queen of the first order. She whirled through life like a comet creating good and destruction in equal measure. You loved her or hated her, but she was not to be ignored. There was a time when her behavior was so outrageous that I did not speak to her for about three years. She was often a public embarrassment. Her shorts were too short and her voice was too loud. She smoked too much and drank too much. Lynn was very wearing on those around her. I always felt free to talk and laugh about Lynn. Hardly anyone in the family mentioned Lynn without rolling their eyes.

On the other hand, Lynn collected and protected abused animals and people. She undertook to care for her disabled grandson. She opened homes for elderly people with dementia, in honor of my grandmother.

Lynn first got breast cancer at age fifty-four. She survived through surgery and chemotherapy and radiation. It took three years to get over what she called "chemo brain," which consisted of very fuzzy thinking and loss of short-term memory. She finally pulled herself together and began life again, a specialty of hers. Lynn got a job working for a real estate company, earned her Realtor's license, and began selling houses. Her life was on track. She was happy and proud of herself.

In June 2006, Lynn's cancer metastasized to her liver. Back she went on chemo. She was totally focused on again dealing with the cancer and getting past it. Because I researched it, I knew that Lynn's prognosis was terrible. Despite that knowledge, I believed that Lynn had fought off the cancer before and would do so again.

In mid-August, I was asked to staff a booth for The Sister Study at a women's health fair in Chicago. The Sister Study is a National Institutes of Health study of the sisters of women who have had breast cancer in an effort to find the causes of the disease. Lynn announced she wanted to drive over from Michigan—about a two-hour drive—to stay overnight with me at the hotel. I agreed, but agreed half-heartedly because I was focused on work, and also because Lynn kept saying, "We can cuddle together!" Argh! No!

Lynn had a full load of chemo and then drove to Chicago. I was shocked by her appearance. She had lost half her hair and a considerable amount of weight. She had bruises covering her arms, neck, chest, and legs. The biggest shock, though, was that she was happy. Maybe for the first time I ever knew her, she seemed clear in her mind about who she was. She had a new favorite song that she insisted I listen to. She said it reflected exactly where she was with life right then. The words were:

I am unwritten,
Can't read my mind,
I'm undefined
I'm just beginning,
The pen's in my hand,
Ending unplanned

Feel the rain on your skin
No one else can feel it for you
Only you can let it in
No one else, no one else
Can speak the words on your lips
Drench yourself in words unspoken
Live your life with arms wide open
Today is where your book begins
The rest is still unwritten
"Unwritten" by Natasha Bedingfield

It was stunning that in the midst of a fight for her life, Lynn felt she was at the beginning of life. She was "unwritten." Lynn was in a worse position now than she had ever before been. Her life was in danger, yet she was showing me that she saw the world as open, a blank slate, unwritten. Lynn was at peace.

Until that moment, I had been Lynn's big sister and her role model. I was the leader; she was the learner In that moment, however, Lynn was in a place I had never been. She saw something I've never seen, and knew something I've never known. Lynn became the leader, and I was the learner. I was humbled. Lynn and I parted in good spirits, not knowing it was the last time we would see each other.

In early September Lynn developed an infection that spread rapidly throughout her system. She started telling her family, "I'm dying." Those close to her dismissed her dramatic declarations as just more Lynn. We thought that a couple of days in the hospital on antibiotics would clear up the infection, and she would be back to fighting that cancer as she always had.

Lynn died in the hospital on September 6, 2006, just one week after she developed the infection. And here is what I learned. The loss of a loved one has no parallel. I first froze my heart so that I could get through traveling to Michigan, comforting her husband and children, and arranging the memorial service. I seemed reasonable, I hugged people, I cried with people, and I kept a white noise in my head to block the pain.

Then I went home. I thought I was having a nervous breakdown. Shock, disbelief, anger, pain, anguish, loneliness, emptiness. None of those words describe what I felt. I was awash in pain. I was shot through with anguish, guilt, and remorse that I hadn't been there or done more. And I was in disbelief that my larger-than-life sister no longer existed. I cried. I cried for hours a day. I cried at home, in the supermarket, on the street, in my car. I couldn't say the words "my sister died" without dissolving into tears. I still can't.

I went off for a month to an island to grieve for my sister, tired of falling apart without warning in socially inappropriate places. I cried a lot more, I tried to write about Lynn but couldn't, I thought about her life, I thought about our relationship, and I regretted so much. I heard her song everywhere I went—in the car, in the drugstore. I believed that the month away would help me "get over" my grief. I thought I could get through the process and go home and resume life.

I was wrong. While my time away allowed me to grieve more openly and fully, I know now that we don't really get over loss. I still grieve for my sister. While I am told that the intensity will lessen, I will always miss her presence in this world. I will never understand how she could be here one minute and be gone the next. I don't know why she died.

So I am new to loss. Given the age we are, loss will occur more and more often. I see that by experiencing grief fully I am more open and available to others who are grieving. I recognize grief now. I see it in the eyes of others, and I reach out to them. I know that for myself, as horrible as loss is—as horrible as grief is—I am a deeper, more empathetic, more loving person for having experienced it.

YOUR TURN

Discussion Questions:

1. What or whom have you lost? Is loss limited to the loss of a person, or has it taken different forms in you life?
2. What have you learned from loss?
3. Do you know someone who has recently suffered loss? How can you support him or her?

Individual Exercise: *Grieve Your Losses*

1. Make a list of everyone you have lost in your life, whether to death or dissolution of a relationship. Include friends as well as family members.
2. After each person's name, put a number from one to ten that reflects the degree to which you suffer from the loss of the relationship, ten being the most difficult loss for you.
3. Look at the three deepest hurts on your list. Have you grieved the loss of these relationships? Have you allowed yourself to feel the pain of the loss? If not, set aside a day. Think about your relationships with those three people. Think about your loss.
4. Speaking aloud, say goodbye to each person in turn, forgiving whatever needs to be forgiven, or asking forgiveness if need be. Tell each person how they enhanced your life, and thank each for being in your life.

Group Exercise: *Say Goodbye*

You will need a timekeeper for this exercise.

1. Stand in a circle. Each person will choose the most difficult loss in her life, and then look around the circle and find the person who reminds her of the person lost. It doesn't matter if the person lost is a man or a woman. The reminder can be height, personality, facial features.
2. One at a time each person will go stand in front of the person chosen. This is the opportunity to say whatever didn't get said before the person went away. Speak out loud. Your statements need no explanation. Just see the person in front of you and for one minute say what you want to say.
3. When all are complete, go back to your seats, and describe in your notebook the experience of saying goodbye.

Assignment:
Pretend you are the fourth author of *Saving the Best for Last* and write your story about "Loss."

Leaving Normalcy Behind and Not to Our Grandchildren

We are the generation born or raised in the 1950s who came of age in the '60s and early '70s. It felt as though we straddled two disparate worlds, one rooted in conformity, the other in its exact opposite. We were the daughters of our mothers. No matter what our mothers' actual lives were like, they presented us with an idealized picture of what life *should* be like. And, like the dutiful daughters most of us were, we attempted to fulfill that expectation. We planned to marry, have children, and raise happy families. Many of us who chose careers first, went into teaching.

But the '60s and early '70s were, for most of us, an explosion in the middle of Vietnam and the anti-war movement, women's liberation, the civil rights movement, the hippie movement, and the assassinations of John F. Kennedy, Martin Luther King, Malcolm X, and Robert Kennedy. These events all served to turn the predictable world into which we were born and raised into alien territory. We lived in a world our mothers could not have imagined.

The intervening years have been for many of us a strange mixture of the two extremes. We have raised out families as proscribed. But many of our "idyllic" marriages have resulted in divorce, or, at the very least, times of serious questioning about our choices. We may have also questioned our career choices or the abandonment of our careers. Many of us have felt that for decades we have walked a fine line between the world of tradition and the one of possibility.

Now, at midlife and beyond, we get to pause and reconsider. We get to reassess the very notion of "normalcy." For many of us, we get to transition from "normalcy" as safety and security to the knowledge that we are only as safe and secure as we believe ourselves to be. We get to take the leap, trusting ourselves enough to know that where we land will be a better place. And we still get to be proud of and to enjoy the families we have created. Our mothers' generation may have wanted nothing more than that. Our generation wants nothing less.

RENEE

When I raised my children, I wanted them to become loving, self-fulfilled, responsible adults. I also wanted them to be fearless and independent. Unlike the over-protective, fearful environment in which I was raised, I deliberately encouraged their independence. I didn't use a gate at the top of the steps. Instead, I stayed with them while they negotiated the stairs themselves. When they came crying to me with complaints like, "I fell down!" instead of reacting, I would ask, "Why did you do that?" It was my funny way of stopping them in their tracks. They would look at me and say, "Huh?" The tears would be over. I also told them repeatedly that they were capable of succeeding in whatever path they chose in life. I'm proud that my children have, indeed, evolved into adults who are willing to take risks in life, and who see the world as a never-ending adventure, rather than something to be wary about.

In spite of my children's successful transition into adulthood, I have to admit to a certain degree of apprehension about the prospect of becoming a grandparent. I've never been a fan of babies, at least for more time than it takes to coo, "Oh, isn't he/she adorable!" I don't think I'll be good at passing the baby photos around and regaling people with stories about how Little Whoever is potty training. And whining about a cranky baby is acceptable when you are the baby's mother; it doesn't play as well coming from a grandmother.

I'm left to develop my own style of grandparenting, one that will have loving my grandchildren be compatible with staying true to myself. I will take the best of my parenting to give to the grandchildren. I will foster the same sense of independence and excitement about life in them. I will let them know that they are capable of anything—not because they are as smart as Albert Einstein or as beautiful as Catherine

Zeta-Jones or as talented as Tiger Woods—but simply because they *choose* whatever they want in life, and they are willing to work for it.

I would like to be an example of a terrific woman who just happens to be their grandmother. I'd like them to appreciate my humor and know that I can be even sillier than they are. In public, I've been known to crack up at extremely inappropriate moments. When "Heat Wave" or "Me and Bobby McGee" comes on the car radio, I roll up the windows, pound on the steering wheel and sing for dear life. I don't plan on changing any of that by virtue of becoming a grandmother. I will show my grandchildren how to be outrageous, not just in their actions but in their dreams, because sometimes, getting what we want in life means having the nerve to be outrageous.

What I'll leave behind is the constant worry I had with my children that all the little things I'd say or do that were wrong would somehow taint them for life. I'll have enough faith in how I raised my children that my grandchildren will be resilient enough to know that parents and grandparents sometimes make mistakes.

Hopefully, if the grandchildren balk at having such an atypical grandparent, my children will be able to tell them that under the eccentricity, and in spite of some imperfections and much frustration, there was usually a lot of good, solid parenting going on. There was always sound advice. There were always arms to hug, ears to listen, and a heart to care. There was always a wish for them to fly, but solid ground for them to land. And always, there was a commitment that they came first.

JOYCE

Dear Future Grandchildren,

I am writing to you at the urging of your parents, who have thoroughly briefed me about what I did to embarrass them as they were growing up. For your sakes, they request I avoid doing the following in public.

I will refrain from wearing political and/or feminist buttons that might offend you. This will be relatively easy, as I do not know what happened to my button collection. In the event I find it, you will not see me wearing "Down with Capitalism," or "Power to Lesbians."

I will refrain from placing political placards in the windows of my house or bumper stickers on my car that say things like "End the racist killings in Atlanta" or "23 black children dead in Atlanta—what is the establishment doing?" And since I am no longer politically active in the Rainbow Coalition (I was a founding member), I will not run again as a candidate for the Democratic Convention.

I will no longer hold book club meetings in my home where you and your friends might overhear debates on the relative merits of socialism vs. communism vs. capitalism, or discussions about Marxism and Leninism. You will not have to worry that your friends might ask you disconcerting questions about my politics.

I will not live with a female lover. For that matter, I will not live with a male lover. When and if I am ever in a committed relationship with a man, we will live separately so as not to agitate you.

I make these declarations to you about what I will give up. Now let me tell you what you can count on. First, you can be sure that I will act on my convictions. I will continue to do whatever I can to create a just, abundant, compassionate, peaceful planet for all. In that vein, I will continue to fight the HIV/AIDS epidemic and to educate people to prevent the spread of this disease.

I also promise personal gifts. I will always be available to you. There is nothing you could do or say that would shock me, or make me angry. I will be honored with whatever you share with me and will listen with an open mind and heart. I want to hear about your successes, your troubles, your dreams and ambitions. And if you want my support, it is here for the asking.

You can count on my unconditional love, just as I have given it to your parents. There is nothing you could do or say that would cause me not to love you. I may not like or agree with your behavior, but I will love you regardless.

My dear grandchildren, I hope this letter reassures you that I will make every effort not to embarrass you and that you can count on me to be there for you.

Love,

Grandmom

P.S. By the way, I wanted you to know that I started a new button collection you might be interested in. I already have "Support Gay Marriage," "Women For Choice," "No Condom, No Sex," "Seniors Are People Too," "Women For Peace," and a few others...

JEAN

I have six grandaughters and a brand new grandson. My grandaughters range from ages five to thirteen—six little girls who get to be women in an age in which the world has become frighteningly dangerous at both a personal and a global level. Six little girls who will be told by their schools, their churches, their peers, and by every advertising message they see, to be "normal," and to obey authority and the law.

I no longer think these are valid messages to give to little girls. It is the pressure to fit in that leads, at an individual level, to consumerism, teen pregnancies, drugs, and AIDS. It is unquestioning obedience to authority that allows totalitarianism, global war, and poverty to thrive.

I spent most of my life suppressing the urge to be great. I grew up in an era and at an economic level where the primary check on unacceptable behavior was, "Who do you think you are?" Expressed aspirations or unconventional behavior were greeted as an attack on the norm, thus an attack on the family and the values held by the immediate community. I understood that if these thoughts or this behavior continued, my well being, my security, my being loved and accepted would be in jeopardy. It never occurred to me to wonder how the thoughts of an eight year-old could possibly be so worrisome.

I grew up thinking that to stand out, to be different, was unacceptable. There was one exception to the rule. It was okay to stand out through achievement, as long as you didn't act arrogant about it. So, an all "A" report card was great, but being the only student in the school to vote for Thomas Dewey against Dwight Eisenhower in the mock student presidential election was not okay. Winning honors in the piano competition was fine, but racing around on my bike long into the time when my friends were experimenting with eye shadow was not okay.

When I was eighteen and attending a small church-related college in the Midwest, I wrote my parents a letter than I now read as a pretty pitiful wail of a trapped spirit. "I don't want to get married and have children and live in the suburbs!" I wrote. "I want to do something in the world, something that matters, something that adds to humankind!"

Now, it may be important to know that I was at this church college because I had lied to my parents. I had two choices about college: I could go to the local teacher's college (my parents' first choice because I could then live at home with them in New Jersey); or, I could go to Hope College way far away in what seemed to me (at seventeen) to be an exotic place called Michigan. The only way I saw to get to Michigan to widen my world was to lie about my goals, and so I told my parents I wanted to be a missionary.

So, I was a rising junior at the college and watching all the girls around me move ever more quickly toward their Mrs. The not-so-light joke of the time was that the Mrs. was the degree of choice for all of us. I was not moved toward that direction. I had hardly dated, didn't much know what men were about, couldn't imagine committing my life to the service of one, and had longings, pulls, desires, to be someone.

Three months later, I quit college and went home. I got a job as a secretary. I closed down my world and tried to shut down my longings. When the nice young man I had been dating at college asked me to marry him, I said yes. It was what I was supposed to do.

I expended an incredible amount of energy over the next twelve years keeping my unruly self under control. The early 1960s passed me by because I was busy fitting in by being married and having children. The Peggy Lee song "Is That All There Is?" played through my mind unbidden as I was nursing my children and teaching Sunday school. I was going to be normal if it killed me.

For me, it was the civil rights movement that blasted me out of my quest for normality. I was a minister's wife in Mobile, Alabama, when Martin Luther King, Jr. was assassinated. Riots threatened and the church leaders in Mobile, black and white, searched for ways to reach out, to calm, to grow, to understand. Meanwhile, in my husband's church, it was discovered that the uncle of Coretta Scott King, Mr. Alfred Scott, had "insinuated himself into our midst" (our midst being the middle of an all-white church) by being the church janitor for forty years. He revealed himself by asking for time off to go to the funeral.

Immediately there were more than rumblings of "Fire him!" or "If we had known...," and "There is a viper in our bosom!" Many felt that Mr. Scott had purposely hidden his connection to Dr. King. Most of the people, until this event, hadn't known Mr. Scott's last name, because, in the practice of white people in the South at that time, servants were known by first name only. For forty years, the church members had only known Mr. Scott as Alfred.

Well, it didn't take a road to Damascus experience for me to get it. Lightening simply struck. The utter evil of the system overwhelmed me. The totally bravery of the civil rights leaders humbled me. Dr. King had lived for far more than himself. He had no desire to be normal and every desire to be a shining leader to free his people from hatred, disrespect, and violence. Alfred Scott had just imperiled his forty-year job to honor and support Dr. King and his family. Many, many people, male and female, were giving their hearts, time, energy, and yes, even their lives to the great purpose of human understanding. They were not striving to be normal. They didn't give a damn about normality. They had a larger reason for living.

Mr. Scott did not get fired, and he came back and completed putting his children through college before he retired. I don't doubt that his final years there were even less comfortable than his first forty, given the new suspicion and distrust that took residence in the church. Nevertheless, he did what he needed to do. He was a hero to me.

I, too, scrapped normality. I took to the streets in the civil rights movement. I became passionate and active about the rights and roles of women. I went back to college and got my degree. I worked on the McGovern campaign. I dragged my kids to rock concerts, and political organization meetings and parties. I got divorced from the lovely man who had not bargained for the "me" I was becoming. I went to law school and worked three jobs to support my family. And, I became a civil rights lawyer. For the next twenty years I wrote Federal policy on issues about the desegregation of public schools, the rights of girls to play sports, and the rights of kids with disabilities in the public schools. My parents and church and community tried to do right by me, but Mr. Alfred Scott taught me what made life worth living.

I have realized it isn't about the "doing-ness" of it all. The things I did are not what matters. What does matter is that I was (and am) passionate, energetic, seeking, inquiring, giving, loving, and working toward something larger than I. Have I screwed up along the way? Absolutely. Was I a great mother? I don't think so. Did I do things I regret? Oh yes, oh yes. But I have been identifying and living my passion. I have been seeking and fulfilling what the universe meant for me to do here on earth. I am anything but normal.

My grandchildren love me, and they think I am strange. That is just great. That is as it should be. It is my job to model for them, to provide for them an alternative to "fitting in." So if anyone ever says to one of them, "Who do you think you are?" they can simply say, "I'm my grandmother's granddaughter."

YOUR TURN

Discussion Questions:

1. What do you think is the purpose of life? What is the purpose of *your* life?

2. What are the benefits of conforming to social expectations? What are the costs?

3. What would it take for you to be a role model for your children and grandchildren?

Individual Exercises:

Exercise One: *Find Your Vision*

In your notebook, write three full pages. Each line will begin "My vision for my life is…".Do not stop to think, just write as fast as you can. You will find after about two pages your creative self will take over from your analytical self. You may be surprised by what emerges.

Exercise Two: *Letting Go of Normal*

1. Who are your heroes? List in your notebook three people whom you deeply admire.

2. Describe the qualities that make them heroes to you. Describe the ways in which you are like them.

3. Are any of them "normal?" Did they fit in? Did they care what people thought about them? Would stepping out of the norm like they did frighten you? If so, why? How are you like them?

Group Exercise: *What We Really Want*

1. Form a circle with one person in the center. The question to be answered by the person in the center is, "What do you want most in your life?" The person in the middle starts saying what she wants, for example, "I want love, I want peace, I want to contribute. I want to write books."

2. The job of the people in the circle is to constantly ask the person "What do you want? What do you want? What do you want?" People should all speak at once, and the louder the question is asked the better, because the purpose is to get the middle person out of her left brain and into her creative, authentic self.

3. Keep asking the question until the people in the circle believe that what is coming out of the person in the center is truly what that person wants.

4. As each person completes her time in the center, she will write down in her journal what it is she wants and then rejoin the circle.
5. This continues until everyone has had a turn in the center.
6. The group then comes together to discuss what opened up for them during this exercise about what they *really* want.

Assignment:

Pretend you are the fourth author of *Saving the Best for Last* and write your story about "Leaving Normalcy Behind" in your notebook.

Shifting Gears

We call this chapter "Shifting Gears" partly out of homage to the manual shift transmission cars in which we all learned to drive. Driving those old cars for the first time, many of us experienced a profound sense of fear. Would we damage the car? Would we damage ourselves? Would we get lost? Would we do something stupid and get a ticket? Would we have to spend the rest of our lives only riding bikes?

Shifting gears through life, whether by changing profession or location or lifestyle, causes much the same apprehension. Will we damage the lives of others? Will we damage our own lives? Will we get lost? Will we do something stupid and lose all our money? Will we spend the rest of our lives regretting our decision?

In our cars, after the fears subsided and we were moving along, the road stretched before us, and only we were in control of where it would take us. The same held true for our lives. Only by shifting were we able to move. So we shifted. And we shifted. And we may have to shift again. The ability to shift a stick may be rapidly becoming a lost art, but the ability to shift gears in life remains a talent we have used over and over. And we will shift as many times as necessary to travel the roads we need to travel to get to where we want to go.

RENEE

I became obsessed with visual perspective when I was about four years old. I wanted to draw a table, but could only manage a circle with a bunch of lines radiating from it. It didn't match actual tables I saw with my eyes. The problem drove me crazy, so much so that one night

I couldn't sleep. I got out of bed, picked up a crayon and made repeated attempts to draw tables on the inside door of the wooden wardrobe in my bedroom. My parents didn't appreciate the manner in which I chose to express my budding creative talent.

In defiance of a decided lack of any kind of serious creativity on the part of my family (with the possible exception of my mother's uncanny ability to sculpt large swans out of chopped liver), I was always into something. I wrote, I drew, I painted, I danced. I scattered my thoughts across pages, my visions across canvasses, and my body across wooden floors. Whatever experiences life handed to me, they were always more clearly processed when I transitioned them from my brain to my hands or my feet.

In spite of my love of the arts, I believed that I didn't have the necessary talent or perseverance to compete as a professional artist. I also listened to my mother, who told me that being a teacher was the best profession for a woman. So I opted to major in Special Education in college. I completed my student teaching experience at a state institution for the mentally retarded. I filled pages and pages of my notebook with poems about the kids I taught.

Shortly before my first child was born, I enrolled in an Adult Ed oil painting class. I attended religiously. I missed one class the week I gave birth. The next week, I was back in class.

During my loony years of early motherhood, my creative processes slowed down but never stopped. I continued to paint, to write and to fashion outrageous Halloween costumes for my children with whatever was around the house.

When my marriage began its slow but relentless slide toward oblivion, my ability to process rational thought was the first casualty. Fear, anger, desperation, confusion all took up residence in the main part of my brain, seemingly wiping out everything that had been there before. I felt like a blind person who came home one day, only to discover that someone had rearranged all the furniture in my absence.

Although it seemed that creativity disappeared entirely, it was not so. Behind the scenes, my brain was furiously trying to make sense of what was happening in my life. Since I couldn't resolve the issues that were facing me, my unconscious took over and began to resolve them for me in another form.

I accompanied my husband on a business trip to San Francisco. While he was in meetings, I walked to Fisherman's Wharf, sat down on the pier, and, with no thought in my head other than observing and enjoying the goings on, I began to pull scraps of paper from my purse and to scribble what appeared to be random, out-of-control sentences. Within a half hour, I had exhausted the empty space on all sales receipts and credit slips that were squirreled away in my purse.

A short time later, on a family camping trip, I locked myself in the minivan and began writing sentences, then paragraphs in a spiral notebook. I was starting to become a bit concerned with my erratic literary behavior. When we returned from the trip, I retrieved all of the receipts, credit slips, and the notebook, and I sat in front of the typewriter and stared at what I thought was the solid evidence of my dementia. I had a choice: burn the evidence, or turn it into something.

I wrote each night until one or two in the morning. I wrote with the same intensity that compels people to run marathons or climb mountains. The result was a novel, a fictionalized version of my frustrations, my fantasies, and my idealized future. It was a very bad novel, but a novel nonetheless. I had transformed from an occasional writer of short stories and poetry into a novelist. And all it took was my life falling apart.

I continued to write throughout my forties. I had some short stories published in literary magazines. I produced another novel, much better than the first. I began to think of myself as a writer. I let go of the painting. For me, writing allowed me to plumb my creative capabilities at a deeper level. It was also something that could be done anywhere, anytime when the inspiration hit. And, when I finally got over my morbid fear of word processing, words flew out at a sometimes alarming rate.

In my fifties, I made the decision to become more rigorous about my craft. I joined a writers group. I enrolled in an intensive writing seminar. At age fifty-five, I was invited to participate in a group reading. I'm terrified of public speaking. I assumed that reading something very personal to me would be even worse than making a speech. I would be baring my soul and my talent to a group of strangers. The thought was enough to make me run to the bathroom.

When the evening came, I walked to the front of the room and sat at a small table. I began to read the introductory chapter of my third novel. The feeling was unlike any I had ever had before. The room was completely silent, but I could hear people *listening*. They were listening to the words I had written. When I finished, there were a few moments of silence and then people applauded. At the end of the evening, people came up to me to tell me how much they had enjoyed my work. I was honored and humbled. The feeling was pure joy.

I note the difference between my writing since turning fifty and my writing before. It mirrors the total change in my life when I made a conscious decision to take myself on at my fiftieth birthday. My goal was to become "better" each year, to take on new physical and mental challenges, to expand both my inner and outer horizons.

My creative writing has done more to achieve this goal than anything else I have ever done after age fifty. My writing has, at times, been my yoga, my meditation, my therapy, my best friend. My writing has allowed me to go deeper into my life, while at the same time going further with it.

On paper, I can take my characters as far as I wish them to go. Or, more often, they decide to go places I never thought of (or was afraid to go) and they take me along. Not only do I learn about them, I learn about myself. On paper, the complexities of human behavior which made no sense to me in my childhood, or which make little sense to me in my adulthood, suddenly make perfect sense. On paper, I am able to say what in my past I was too afraid or too angry or too confused to say. On paper, I can continue to pour out love and acknowledgment to those long gone. On paper, I can love and honor those I bypassed, those I never recognized as having been the great forces they were in my life.

More importantly, my writing has allowed me to listen. I am able to listen to the wisdom of others that I couldn't "hear" before. I am able to listen to my own wisdom, which I now know to be profound, in those magical moments when I can put the world and my immediate concerns aside.

In my childhood and teens, I defined growth as taller, bigger, stronger. In my twenties and thirties, I defined it as accumulating the characteristics of adulthood: the marriage, the family, the profession. In my forties, growth went inward, and took the form of self-exploration. Growth for my fifties and sixties is self-expression.

I have chosen to write, and I am blessed with the joy that has ensued. Other women I know have discovered similar joy and fulfillment in painting, in weaving, in sculpting, in fashioning pottery. Just as our children gestated inside of us until the moment they chose to present themselves to the world, our artwork does the same. Our energies were young and raw when we produced our children. We now produce artwork that is a result of more mature, tempered energy, but one that is just as boundless. And just as we were grateful beyond measure for the miracle of birth, we are also so for the gift of our creativity.

I am aware that my life after age fifty has already achieved a level of creativity that is deeper, more profound, and more mature than what came before. And, unlike the vagaries of athleticism which often depend on strong, healthy bodies, I am comforted by the knowledge that the creative process often improves as one ages, allowing us to see with a degree of visual acuity that can't be measured by an ophthalmologist. As the notion of our days becomes finite, our creative capacities can become infinite. As the road ahead shortens, the creative process can become more far reaching. As our creative reach expands, our world becomes bigger.

And bigger really *is* better.

JOYCE

I have taken risks in my life, but realized in my fifties that most of those "risks" were calculated ones. In other words, I took risks, but I was reasonably certain that I would succeed. I was never outrageous.

Up to my fifties, many considerations and responsibilities were in my way. I was the sole support of my children. I had to pay the mortgage and put food on the table. I could not be too daring for fear that I would not be able to carry out my obligations as single mother and breadwinner. This was what I told myself.

Not long before I turned fifty, I resigned my position as a high school English teacher. I hadn't planned my resignation. It came at a time when I was in pain from four herniated cervical discs, pain that completely incapacitated me. I couldn't drive, walk, sit, lie down, or move without pain. My doctor urged me to give up teaching and focus on healing. Since I was unwilling to undergo surgery before trying more conservative treatment, it was going to take some time before I would fully regain my health and be able to resume my normal activities. I took the doctor's advice and resigned.

Giving up my career frightened me. My work was not only my identity, but it was my sole source of income. If and when I got well and could work again, I wondered what I would do, where I would find a job. Quitting teaching seemed like a reckless act, a plunge toward an unknown future that I did not want to take.

I felt like a victim. When I made the decision to resign, I felt forced into it. I was angry that I was powerless to the physical pain that crippled me, made it impossible for me to work and to function as a normal person, and made me dependent on others. I was angry at the school system. I believed that part of my back injury was brought on by the daily stress of fighting a complacent administration that cared nothing about its students or teachers. I was also angry that a neck injury I sustained many years earlier continued to be a painful problem I could no longer ignore.

I did not accept what happened to me. I resisted the needs of my body and its pain even when I could no longer ignore it. I did not want to face the effects of stress, pushing myself past my limits, and ignoring the symptoms. Through that year of treatment and counseling with my doctor, I slowly let go of my anger and acknowledged my responsibility for taking care of myself. But my fears about what was going to happen when I got well never went away.

Regardless of my anxiety about where I would land, I got well without surgery and began looking for a new job. I wrote a resume for the first time in my life, began scouring the want ads, told everyone I knew that I wanted a job, and volunteered on a political campaign while I was searching.

A woman who worked with me on the campaign was impressed with my organizing and training skills. After Election Day, she brought a help wanted ad from the *Baltimore Gaypaper*. An HIV/AIDS organization was seeking its first Director of Volunteer Services, and she encouraged me to apply. With some trepidation I sent off my resume and got an immediate response: "When could I come for an interview?"

The interview was not what I expected. Six people, including the executive director, board members, and volunteers drilled me on my knowledge of HIV disease and death and dying. I knew next to nothing, but reminded them the point of the interview was to find someone suitable for working with volunteers and developing programs. I could learn HIV. They hired me.

- The career move did not matter nearly as much as what I learned from the experience. I learned several huge lessons which I took into my fifties and sixties:

- I am strong. I can survive whatever I need to overcome to move on with my life;

- I can start over at any point in my life;

- I can go kicking and screaming, or I can surrender to the flow.

After that first experience of abruptly changing careers, I can't say the changes that came afterwards were easier or less scary. I did, however, become more daring in my risk-taking.

At fifty-one, a friend and I started our own consulting company. We had the great idea that the time had come to train businesses to deal with HIV/AIDS in the workplace. We thought companies needed what we were offering, but they didn't think so. After two years of trying to make a go of it, we had to admit that our business was a failure. During the time we were struggling, I racked up thousands of dollars in debt, both business and personal.

My worst fear had come to pass: I had failed for the first time in my life. Oddly, I was not devastated. I did not feel humiliated. I still lived. I didn't die. I didn't lose any friends. I would repay my debts, and I would move on.

I was surprised to discover I was in celebration that I had finally done what I had always been afraid of doing. And just because my business failed, it did not mean I was a failure. Life went on. I got another job and worked for someone else again.

Later, in my mid-fifties, I decided that it was time to try some new ventures, things I had wanted to do for awhile but had still been afraid to try. I decided to quit my job as development officer, move to another city, and find new work—international work. I had no idea what that would be, or where my job search would take me. But I quit my job and moved anyway. I was ready.

Jean let me live with her for six months rent-free while I searched for work. I lived on unemployment for the first time in my life, barely making ends meet. My family thought I had lost my mind. My ex-husband asked me how I could possibly give up my (safe) job and go off into an unknown, uncertain future. I could only say that the only way I would know what I could do was to give it a shot. Besides, I told him, I could always move back to Baltimore. I wasn't selling my house.

I had already experienced failure, so I wasn't worried. I knew I'd survive. Even the possibility of humiliation from failing again did not stop me from moving.

I also moved for love. I was dating someone steadily for the first time in many years. The prospect of long-distance dating did not intrigue me, and he was not keen on driving to Baltimore; so that, too, was motivation to move from Baltimore to Virginia. My sister asked me what would happen if the relationship didn't work out. My answer was the same one I had given my ex-husband. I wouldn't know if I didn't give it a try. If it didn't work out, I'd survive.

The relationship did not work out. The career move did. With a referral from Jean, I got a gig directing a Polio Eradication Broadcasting Project for the Voice of America. The entire year I worked this contract, I was still looking for a "regular" job.

I left the VOA to take a development and public relations position with a national HIV/AIDS organization, but after a year I knew it was not where I wanted to be; I wanted to go back to being self-employed. But my belief that I should have a contract before resigning stopped me: I had unconsciously reverted to calculated risk taking. I saw that clinging to the security of my current job shut down possibilities. My fear and passivity were holding me back. I mustered up my courage and turned in my letter of resignation.

The day after my resignation, my former supervisor at the VOA called to ask what I was up to. When I told him I had quit my job the day before, he immediately offered me a contract to come back to the VOA to do AIDS work.

Since then, I have been doing exactly what I moved to the Washington area to do. I am self-employed, have interesting, challenging, meaningful work with a number of organizations, and earn more than double what I was earning in Baltimore. I also travel. I once spent several months in East Africa researching and documenting case studies for UNICEF. My experience is of fulfillment and success.

Yet I still have my fears. They never really go away. I worry that I won't be good enough, won't have enough contracts, don't know enough, will make an ass of myself, or be penniless. It doesn't matter what I worry about. What matters is that my fears no longer stop me. I can have my fears and still take action on my dreams.

If I'm successful, that's great. If I fail, that's great, too. I'll just pick myself up and move on.

JEAN

In the autumn of 1999, I was at the pinnacle of my legal/management career. I was fifty-eight years old, and Chief of Staff of a Federal agency that provided support for all federally sponsored international broadcasting.

I hated almost everything about the job. I was the original square peg in a very round hole. Two years later I was consulting internationally, presenting workshops called "Women of a Certain Age," hosting a Web-based radio show called "Women of a Certain Age," and modeling in Washington, D.C., Philadelphia, and New York.

What happened? I reinvented myself.

Reinvention is not merely changing jobs. Reinvention is taking on a way of living and being that is completely new and challenging. It involves leaving the place, be it job or home, or relationship, where you are most comfortable, and striding into the unknown. Reinvention is an exercise in creation. It is frightening, exciting, and awesome.

I have reinvented myself several times, and every time I do it I hear my no-nonsense coal miner forbearers hissing, "Are you crazy?" I remember Greek myths about the costs of hubris, and I shiver in my shoes.

Reinvention involves declaring what it is you are creating next. The scariest thing I can do is to declare that something will happen when I have no earthly notion of how it will happen and seemingly no present ability to make it happen. Yet that is what I do. I have chosen to live as the sole, uncontested author of my life. For me to be the creator of my life, I must claim responsibility for everything *in* my life. The downside of being responsible is that I have no excuses. Nothing can ever be anyone else's fault. The upside is that I believe the universe aligns with declared intentions, so I can declare goals that are well beyond my present abilities and well beyond logic.

When I was unhappy as the Chief of Staff of the International Broadcasting Bureau, I first thought the answer was simply to find a new job. (Even reinvention people forget sometimes that cosmetic changes are not real changes.) I knew I was harboring a notion that I didn't want any job at all, but that was too scary to even think about. I was having trouble grasping the notion of letting go of one source of income before I had another safely in hand.

The fearful side of me kept repeating in my head that I had a lovely home and big mortgage. If I quit before having another job, I would have to live on savings until I got another job. This would risk my house and my future. If I just quit and decided not to find another job, I would have a pension that would kick in, but my income would fall immediately and forever to one third of what it now was. Either way, I could not afford to keep my house.

Besides, I liked my standard of living. I shopped, took cruises, bought presents for my grandchildren. I gave to charity, traveled freely to see my parents, and rented a house at the beach in the summers. I didn't want to risk any of that.

I spent the next several months applying for management jobs at other Federal agencies. As there were few jobs in international broadcasting, I began applying for jobs in my former civil rights management field. While I had loved every bit of work I did in civil rights, and while that field had held my heart and my attention for twenty-two years, the job descriptions and the application process did not excite me. I was headed back into an arena where I had given what I had to give, experienced what there was to experience, and learned what there was to learn. Going into another, similar job was simply living from my past rather than in my future.

I took a deep breath and decided that I would quit before I had anything else lined up. I would leap before I looked. That decision took courage and a stubborn belief that whatever happened, I would be all right. There would go two-thirds of my income. I either would have to make money without taking a new job or reduce my outgo of money, and I didn't yet know how. I knew though, that as long as I was pouring my energies into a job I didn't enjoy, I was not free to create what it was I did want. As long as I limited my vision by holding on to a sure thing—my income—I could not possibly create something totally new.

One morning I woke up and knew. It was time to reinvent myself again. But, who did I want to be, and how did I want to be experiencing my life?

I could not specify a career or job that I wanted next, so instead I identified the elements of who I wanted to be. I knew that I wanted to love what I was doing, to be free to shape my time, to create something new in the world, and to make a difference in the world. I wanted to have fun, and I wanted to live comfortably; but, I was willing to live simply.

Having seen at least the outlines of who I wanted to be, I gave two months' notice that I was taking early retirement. I hyperventilated; my mother asked if I had gone insane, and my daughter said something like, "Here goes Mom again!"

The decision was not without effect on my body and mind. I hardly slept the first night and many nights after that. I hashed and rehashed my decision. I plotted ways to reverse what I had done. I had nightmares of being a bag lady. I pictured co-workers around the water cooler whispering about how poor Jean had lost her house, her car, and her mind. I was filled with fear.

I am glad that I gave myself two months for the change to happen. It gave me time to transition out effectively from my position at the broadcasting agency. It also gave me time to dream about what might be next. Most of all, however, it gave the universe the opportunity to demonstrate support for what I was doing.

The moment I gave notice that I was leaving the workplace, things started to happen. First, for reasons beyond my understanding, the phrase "women of a certain age" kept popping into my head. I didn't know why, but I knew that my future was somehow tied to it. I knew that it had to do with creating something new and making a difference in the world. I started talking with other women in my workplace about what it was like to be over fifty, to be women of a certain age. What were their dreams? What were their goals? What was next in their lives? I found women having the same conversations that all of us women had when we were twenty: what shall we do with our lives?

At around the same time, I saw an article in the local newspaper about a start-up Internet radio station that was playing a lot of original music, but also was beginning to broadcast original talk shows. I wrote to them suggesting a show called "Women of a Certain Age." Since I was talking to women over fifty, why not do so for the world to hear? I would interview women over fifty about their lives and their dreams. The radio station owners loved the idea. There was no money in it immediately, but it moved forward my interest in making a difference in the world. It took only three months to get the show on the air.

About two weeks before my last day of work, a television commercial came on that said, "So you want to be a model?" "Well, why not?" I thought. I knew no one in the field and had no experience as a model. That was the very reason I should do it. Why not reinvent myself as a model? What a great demonstration that would be of the potential of women of a certain age. The more I thought about it, the more perfect it became. It was cosmic logic: I would become a model to be a model. I would model facing fears. I would model choosing quality of life over money. I would model making life-changing decisions after fifty.

I immediately did what it is I do when I identify a dream that seems impossible to fulfill: I go public. In this case, I walked out into the hallway of my office and said to the first five people I saw, "I've decided to become a model." For me, that very public pronouncement (which made the rounds of the office in quick order) served several purposes. First, it committed me to the vision. The last thing I want is to be publicly embarrassed. That meant there was no reversing field. I had to follow through.

Second, a public commitment to a dream makes it real for me, and I mean *really* real. The idea is somewhat similar to an athlete envisioning winning the race. I perform a trick in my brain in which I see my vision as already a reality. Thereafter, I never think or say, "I want to be a model," or "I'm going to try to be a model." What I think is, "I am a model." For public consumption, I say that I've decided to become a model, but in my brain it is a done deal.

This "envisioning the dream as real" is an important step because once something already exists, obstacles that appear in my path are just that: obstacles to be overcome. Obstacles cease to be showstoppers because I know that my vision is already in existence. If I had said, "I'm going to *try* to be a model" and the first three modeling agencies I saw said, "Sorry, not interested," it would have been easy for me to be discouraged and quit. With my mind set on the fact that I already was a model, however, those three agencies simply became my first steps toward that goal.

About a week before my last day of work, the agency I had just retired from asked if I would consider working part-time, at home, on my own schedule, on a contract to complete a project begun under my supervision. The contract would last at least six months. There came a source of income, at least for a while.

Shortly after my last day of work, I asked Joyce, who was then living in an apartment, whether she had any interest in moving in with me as a paying roommate. We had lived together earlier for six months and got along just great. She surprised me by saying yes. She wanted to economize and moving in with me made sense to her. There came a source for twenty-five percent of my mortgage payments.

Within a year, I was asked to be a civil rights consultant to an international radio broadcaster headquartered in Prague. This meant performing some work at home on my computer and at least three trips a year to Prague. Oh yes, the perfect contract in the most beautiful city in the world.

I will restate that it was only after I identified the life I wanted and after I replaced my value on security with my value on being who I wanted to be that "women of a certain age" and modeling and new sources of income appeared in my life. One way of viewing this phenomenon is to say that the universe stepped up to support me once I took action, once I identified my dream, and faced my fear. Another way to view it is that clearing my head and heart of concerns about my day-to-day living, and facing and dealing with my fears, freed up energetic space so that creativity could occur.

One year after I declared my vision to become a model for the concept of women of a certain age, I got my first modeling job. The job was for a company that wanted to promote the "healthy after fifty" lifestyle, and they chose me for it.

Of course they did. I am, after all, a model. I model reinvention.

YOUR TURN

Discussion Questions:

1. If we are not doing what we want to do in life, what is keeping us from it?

2. Can we risk our financial well being to pursue our vision for our lives? Can we risk the financial well being of others, like family members, to pursue our vision for our lives? Why or why not?

3. Does getting older affect our ability to make career or other big changes in our lives? In what ways? How can we move forward in spite of that?

Individual Exercises:

Exercise One: *What Stops Us*

In your notebook, answer the following questions. Answer in as much detail as possible.

- Something I really want in my life is …
- I'm afraid to go for it because …
- I am willing to risk the following to have it:

Exercise Two: *Face a Fear*

1. Pick a fear that you have. The fear does not have to be related in any way to your vision. Your fear may be of skydiving or of public speaking or something else entirely.

2. Since facing one fear empowers you to face others, declare your intention, by a specific date, to face this fear.

3. Then do it.

Group Exercises:

Exercise One: *There Must Be Fifty Ways...*

1. Line up at one end of the room.

2. Each person, in turn, must cross the room. No one can cross the room in the same way used by anyone else. If you have fewer than ten people, everyone should go twice.

3. When everyone has had her turn(s), discuss what was learned from this exercise.

    - Could any one individual have thought of all the ways that were used?
    - Was any particular way superior or inferior to any other?

- Does this exercise reveal anything about the unlimited ways there are to reach a goal?
- Does the exercise reveal anything about the value of team and the value of getting support?

Exercise Two: *Solving Problems*

1. The group will sit in a circle.
2. One volunteer will state to the group a vision she has, *e.g.*, she wants to create a farm setting for rescued animals. She then will relate what she sees as a barrier to having her vision, *e.g.*, she doesn't have enough money to obtain the farm.
3. Each person in the circle will, in turn, give a suggestion to the volunteer as to how to approach or solve her problem. The job of the volunteer is just to listen, with no comment, to the suggestions. If the group is small, then go twice around the circle with suggestions.
4. When the exercise is complete, discuss the differences between working alone and getting support for your vision.

Assignment:

Pretend you are the fourth author of *Saving the Best for Last* and write your story about "Shifting Gears" in your notebook.

Friendship

For many of us, friendships change throughout the years, depending on where we are in our lives. We may connect first with the little girl next door, since next door is as far as our tiny world allows. Seamlessly, our world expands, from next door to the block, then on throughout assorted schools, sports teams, offices, interest groups. As our eyes stretch across the ever-widening borders of our world, they land on other women who become an integral part of it. Those of us who put profession first may find others who do so as well. Those of us who make the shift to parenthood find others who share with us the joy, the frustration, the potty training tips. These women, if not lifelong friends, are, at the very least, the women we count on to get us through the days.

For others, friends are the constant in an ever-shifting and sometimes overwhelming and frightening world. Parents, husbands, and children may hurt us, may disappoint us, may leave us. Friends offer more than consolation. They are the soft landing we crave. They are also the evidence we need that we, too, can be what they are.

As many of us age, the friendships we create take on a new dimension. We make the shift from friendships as shared experience to the sense that we are part of a community of women that has no specific interest, or goal, or geographic boundary to identify us. We have simply our age. We are women at midlife and beyond. We have passed through whatever experiences we have chosen or have been chosen for us. We have spent our energies on others and have discovered that there is energy left for ourselves or for the world, whichever we choose. We have formed, and sometimes reformed, families. We have survived, and we have failed more times than we can recall. In the process, we have learned to let go all expectations except the ones we create.

RENEE

I used to think that nobody had anything new to tell me about the meaning of friendship. Without sisters around, I depended on my friends for everything. I always had lots of friends and I always made friends easily. My friends explained to me the mysteries of kissing, dating, sex, and drugs, topics my parents never touched upon. When all other girls around me started menstruating, only my best friend and I were left in our pre-pubescent state. We made a pact, deciding that the only benefit to not reaching womanhood was that we couldn't get pregnant. Therefore, we would be happily promiscuous. Until that moment, I had never experienced more than kissing a boy, much less entertained the prospect of sex. If a boy had approached me with anything sexual in mind, I would have fled. But the secret pact made me feel better. At least I had a plan, and my best friend and I were in it together.

My friends knew my deepest secrets and my darkest fears. When I discovered I was in love with the man who would become my husband, I told it first to a friend before I told it to him. Years later, when I no longer loved him, another friend heard the news before he did. When my first child screamed all day and shattered my fantasy notion of what motherhood would be like, I told two friends about my misery. One comforted me because her son was even worse. The other, still unmarried, loved me in such an unconditional way that I believed her when she said everything would be all right. That same friend was dying when my marriage was falling apart. The final words spoken between us were not me telling her that I loved her. She knew that. The final words were her telling me that everything would ultimately be okay in my life.

Friendship in my forties meant unconditional love and support. My friends took my concerns seriously and they advised me when I needed advice. They celebrated with me when I succeeded, and they commiserated with me when I failed. What they never did was to make demands on me that I didn't believe I could fulfill. That wouldn't have fit into the paradigm of what I believed friendship to be. All that changed around the time my marriage was coming apart.

Unhappy as I might have been in my marriage, my married state at least gave me an identity, a grounding. When I became single, I literally didn't know who I was anymore. I chose not to be around friends who were happily married. If I was flailing, I wanted to be around others who were doing so as well. If I was miserable, I sought out women who were also miserable. I cared only about telling my story and justifying my actions, actions I was ashamed of. The only way I could think of to make my actions less shameful was to share them with others who understood.

I became a master at telling my story: My husband was controlling. My husband was arrogant. My husband was not thoughtful. My husband was oblivious to my wants and needs. I had no choice but to look elsewhere for understanding and affection. My "friends" listened. They shook their heads in sympathy. They shared their own misery, their own shameful actions with me. It was perfect. We were members of an unnamed and undeclared club of victims, and I was the queen. I wallowed in my reign for several years. The only problem with this scenario was that my life wasn't moving forward.

In 1995, at the age of forty-eight and three years after my ex-husband and I separated, I enrolled in a workshop created to allow people to see their lives in a new, objective way. We would see what was working and what wasn't working, and we would obtain the tools necessary to live from our vision rather than from our circumstances. I said I wanted to change. I didn't want to be a victim anymore. But secretly, I just wanted to continue to tell my story and to justify my actions.

The workshop was hard, really hard. No one wanted to hear my story. Worse, nobody *cared* about my story. How was this possible? I spent a lot of time struggling, and a lot of time crying. Nobody cared about that, either. At one point, I left the room. I had never walked out like that on anything in my life. (My marriage didn't count. I was a victim, remember?).I came back after sobbing for thirty minutes in the ladies room.

Slowly, I realized that these people in the workshop cared about me in a way that I had never experienced before. They didn't care about my story or my justifications. They held me to a higher possibility. That was an entirely too frightening concept for me. I wanted the old version of friendship back. Worse, I suspected that their version of me was far too powerful. I simply wasn't capable of being who they believed me to be. Secretly, I believed the successful businesswoman, mother, and PTA president was a failure, not some powerful woman who could take full responsibility for her life.

The people in the workshop were unstoppable. They expected me to be a leader. And that wasn't simply a person who led PTA meetings but instead someone who was a visionary and an example. Someone who would never be a victim under any circumstance. Someone who lived her life in an empowering way and who was a stand for others to do so as well. I hated these people. Unbelievably, these people didn't care that I hated them. They stood their ground. They held me to my highest possibility, even when my highest possibility was the last place where I wanted to be.

The workshop introduced me to a version of friendship I had never considered before, one that looked more like "tough love" but was truly a new definition of unconditional love and support. It centered around responsibility rather than commiseration. My friendships with Joyce and Jean came out of the workshops and with them, I operated within the new paradigm of friendship. We declared our visions to each other. We took responsibility for our actions. We never treated each other as victims. We called each other on behavior we felt didn't serve us. It was relatively easy until we decided to write the book, and then for me, everything started to unravel again.

When we started to write the book, I quickly reverted to my old behavior patterns. Once again, I had my resume: I was the real writer of the group. I had written. I had been published. I had experience with how the world of publishing operated. For a while, it worked. Like maybe for about five minutes. Within no time at all, each of them was critiquing my writing, and I was unprepared to accept the comments. Worse, the standard they expected of me was far more demanding than being the strongest writer in the group: I was to be honest about myself and about them. To write about certain experiences or topics was sometimes too painful and too difficult, and to accept that the writing might be less than my best effort was unsettling. And then, to give honest feedback to them under the same impossible circumstances was just too much.

In addition to the writing, there was the minutia around publishing and marketing the book. It seemed to me there was a bottomless pit of decisions to be made, and Jean and I disagreed on everything. I took every disagreement personally. I saw Jean as a force of nature and so every one of her opinions that varied from mine was a slap in my face.

Having an editor was even more difficult. I wanted winks and secret signals. *"I see that you are the best writer. Your work needs so little improvement."* This was not to happen. I was given as many rewrites as Joyce and Jean, sometimes more. By the time the manuscript was completed, I felt as though I could no longer depend on the one talent I thought I had. And I seriously reconsidered a friendship that kept forcing me ever farther away from feelings of self-satisfaction and comfort.

I couldn't get rid of Jean no matter how much I tried. She was steadfast. She told me one day that ours was the first friendship she felt totally committed to, and the thought terrified her. She had no idea of how terrified I was to hear her words.

I continue to struggle daily with comfort versus possibility. Jean, Joyce, and I continue to write. Jean and I continue to disagree. I continue to feel trapped between the desire to avoid conflict and the desire to speak my mind. But what is at the heart of it all is my belief that, even in the mildest of situations, I feel that it is my ego that is at stake. Disagreement of any kind is personal, and showing vulnerability means raw exposure and potential attack. I am on guard. I want to put up my shield.

The concept of a healthy ego is new ground for me. My penchant for sliding back into a victim mode shuts down any potential for growth; a healthy ego enables me to trust myself enough to be vulnerable to others and to hear the value in feedback or in other opinions as a way to reach higher and stretch further, rather than hearing it as a criticism that shuts me down.

I have now (again) added this new dimension of vulnerability to friendships. I understand that I have to get over myself, and I don't like to get over myself. Ever. But I need to get over myself in order to become my *best* self. I understand now that my friends will help me get there. I just have to let go and trust them. Better yet, I have to trust myself. I have to believe in the "me" that they can see so clearly. That's the hard part. And I have far more at stake here than a book.

Joyce

My friends have taught me many important things throughout my life. Jackie, a friend from seventh grade, taught me to smoke. Judy taught me to use tampons and introduced me to jazz, comedian Shelley Berman, the "in" places to hang out in Baltimore, and exotic drinks to imbibe. She also coerced me into going to a picnic where I met my husband-to-be. (Thus, Judy is indirectly responsible for my having a son and daughter.) When I lived with my friend Jean while starting my new career in Washington, D.C., she taught me that I can live with someone and enjoy it—and the person doesn't have to be exactly like me.

In high school I remember having lots of girlfriends, but I realize now that while I believed they were good friends and that we were close, I never revealed much about my home life or my thoughts to any of them. We were friends without knowing anything about each other except the obvious. We talked about boys and makeup and popular music and what to wear to the prom. When one of my church friends told me she was having sex with her boyfriend, I was shocked—I think mostly because she chose to tell me. I couldn't even question her, or talk about it, because it was already too much information for me to handle.

Fast forward forty years from high school to the women's movement and beyond. Jackie and I hadn't seen each other in years. She wrote me this past year on the *Invisible No More* Web site to say that while trying to track me down, she discovered our book. After she read it, she wrote me a long, touching email to say how sorry she was that she had known nothing about what I went through when I was growing up, and how she wished she could have helped me. I wrote back and told her that I couldn't ask for help when I didn't know I needed it. Besides, I was unable to share my experiences at that time. Some friends like Jackie knew from neighborhood gossip or the newspaper that my father was in prison and why, but that was as far as the information went. I never revealed the details of my experiences. I wasn't ready to be that vulnerable.

I held on to most of my deepest secrets until I wrote this book with Jean and Renee. The biggest gift for me is that our writing process deepened our friendship as we struggled through writing, publishing, and promoting our book around the country. We have often told audiences about how hard it was, and still is sometimes, to be completely honest and authentic. We have had to challenge each other to get to the bottom line of our experience: the truth of who we really are in the sharing of our stories.

When Jean, Renee, and I published our book, I worried about how my sisters would react to my personal disclosures. But I worried in vain. In reality, the book opened up an opportunity for us to talk and share thoughts we'd never spoken before. We began to disclose to one another our thoughts on our childhood experiences whereas previously we had acted as if they didn't exist or never happened. We could discuss—and reveal—our own truths and what really matters to us. The four of us have always encouraged and supported one another, but the closeness I experience now is different. My sisters have actually become my friends.

This year Jackie from junior high and Patricia, whom Jackie and I met in college, got together for the first time in forty-four years and spent a week together in California at Patricia's mountaintop home. Jackie and Patricia last saw each other at my wedding when we were twenty-one. We didn't do a lot of sightseeing. We simply spent each day together talking, eating, laughing, and reminiscing. Patricia's husband John cooked for us while we hung out together. We went to the movies, combed through our yearbooks, talked politics, and traded stories about our families and grandchildren.

This trip was yet another reminder of how women, once we bond, are bonded forever. Here we were, three women who hadn't spent any time together in four decades, acting just like we did in college as though no time had passed. The vacation was a time of pure relaxation and fun with the "girls," but it was much more for me. I got to appreciate again how blessed I have been with my friendships and how much they enrich my life.

Men are a different story. I have not had much luck with friendships with straight men, and I used to think it was the fault of the men. This is simply an observation, but to me it seems they don't really know how to be friends, at least not like women, and inevitably they always want sex.

It's their nature (at least that's what many men have told me), but I find it difficult to be myself with men who say (or pretend) they want to be friends. I am a warm, demonstrative person, and I think my warmth—say I hug a guy—is sometimes misinterpreted and leads the man to leap to the conclusion that I have sex on my mind when I simply want to be friendly. My three brothers are just about the only straight men I consider to be my friends, men in whom I can confide and trust.

The male friends I do have are gay. My gay friends are so much easier and more fun to be with. I can let my guard down and simply enjoy whatever we do without worrying about being misinterpreted.

The lasting friendships, my most meaningful relationships, have spanned decades of my life. My friends and I know now what it means to be a friend—in both the giving and receiving. Like all intimate relationships, our friendship engages us in mutual sharing, respect, honesty, and trust. And our sharing has a much deeper context now than the exchange of information and stories like we did when we were teenagers. Our sharing is the gut-level, authentic revealing of who we are: our experiences, feelings, thoughts, and fears. I accept that friendship—like intimacy—calls for complete honesty and truthfulness and vulnerability.

I know that my friends will not abandon me or leave me as I age. Just as they have been there over the years, I feel secure in our friendships and know that they will continue to appreciate me as much as I do them. They choose me as friend, fully accepting me without judgment.

I have a vision of what we girlfriends will be like in the next twenty to thirty years. Without a doubt, I know we will continue to deepen our relationships as we age, and, as we face new losses, experience less independence, or develop infirmities that perhaps restrict our ability to live alone, we will be there for each other as we always have. We will create new ways of surviving and thriving by combining resources, sharing living quarters, or creating communes like we did in the 1960s and 1970s.

Friends take care of friends: it is an implicit, unspoken agreement like no other.

JEAN

When I was a child, there could only be one best friend. Girls came in "twos," and the world revolved around this one person. There was a clear boundary between your best girlfriend and other friends. You sat with your best friend at lunchtime. Your best friend taught you pig Latin, the five ballet positions, and let you try on all her clothes.

My best friend was Eileen. Eileen was there the first day of kindergarten, and our friendship held strong through eighth grade. Over nine years, she was the one who knew my secrets and my insecurities. She was the one who laughed at my foibles and loved me anyway. Eileen and I started the ninth grade at the regional high school. We took the school bus every morning where we got ready for our day, gossiping, laughing, bonding. We hung out after school and all day Saturdays.

Then disaster struck. His name was Joe. One day I had a best friend, and the next day I didn't. Joe became Eileen's best friend. Joe was three years older than we were, a prestigious senior, and he drove Eileen to school and picked her up after school every day. On the weekends they did whatever boyfriends and girlfriends did. I didn't have a clue what that might be. All I knew was that Eileen was gone, and I was bereft.

I found new friends. We had a good time for the rest of high school doing all the things teenage girls in that era did, which mostly involved talking about boys, calling up boys, and driving by boys' houses. But I did miss having a best friend.

It was only later in college that I began to understand that it was going to be women who got me through life. Men might become my primary other, but men were not the go-to people when I needed to talk about problems, issues, or dilemmas that were facing me. We females talk through emotional issues, and we use each other as sounding boards for trying out new ideas or exploring fears.

By college, I also realized it wasn't necessary to have a "best" friend.

As a child, I wasn't sure that I would be accepted in the new, scary world of school. A best friend was protection against rejection. So I expanded my world to girlfriends plural. In high school it happened by accident. Now it happened by choice. I loved having girlfriends. It was like a smorgasbord in that there were girlfriends who just wanted to have fun, girlfriends who were great study buddies, and girlfriends who loved to party. There were even girlfriends who wanted to discuss whether god existed and whether there was such a thing as a strict code of morality sent from heaven. And god knows, all of us wanted to talk about sex.

While we girls talked to each other 24/7, we didn't necessarily tell each other the truth—or at least not all of the truth—about the really important things in our lives. I know now that within my circle of girlfriends one had been molested by her father, one had an abortion in high school, one's mother was a drunk, and one tried suicide at age sixteen. They didn't share that then. I think it was too scary for them to share those secrets. Social acceptance seemed a fragile thing, and those were the days when nobody ever talked about such things. They were considered family secrets. So we didn't share everything. We weren't perfect friends yet, but we were practicing.

My middle years were girlfriendless. There were several reasons for this. First, my husband and I moved a lot—five states in five years— which made it hard to form any lasting friendships. Second, having children was like acquiring a religion. Everything revolved around them, all talk was of them, and there seemed no room for creating friendships. Further, the cult of marriage then required total "loyalty" to one's spouse. The two of you were the unit. All important things were discussed there, if anywhere. This one person you had married had to become the all in all. I spent most of my twenties and early thirties being miserable. I felt I was turning to stone. The lack was not in my husband who is a fine man. Rather, I believe men just aren't wired to provide the same types of friendship that women provide.

The world shifted greatly when, in the following decade, the women's movement burst onto the scene and into my life. "Sisterhood is powerful." Wow! What a concept. The possibility of having friends in unlimited numbers was intoxicating. We were no longer girlfriends; we were sisters. Groups formed everywhere. In those groups we returned to the thing we knew best. We talked. And we talked. And we talked. We let out our secrets, and I mean we really let out our secrets. We shared what we had learned, we cried in each others' arms, and we marched shoulder to shoulder in demonstrations.

It was a heady time. My children no longer went to play dates, they went to political demonstrations. Mothers' coffee klatches were abandoned for rock concerts. And, truth be told, hot chocolate was replaced with marijuana brownies. It was an unbelievably pure time. One that we may never see again in our or our children's' lifetimes. I am so grateful that I lived then—that I woke up—that I learned to give, love, and share. And I learned a whole new definition of friendship.

The women's movement opened the possibility that all women were connected. A global sisterhood. For the first time, I saw that I am connected to my neighbor, to women in Darfur, to women in China. I saw that our common experiences as women were far greater than the differences in our races, religions, or cultures.

In my fifties, friendship took yet another turn. Friendships deepened as life presented us with new challenges: divorces, the death of family members, breast cancer, wayward children. It is as though we have been practicing the art of friendship for years just so that it can now flower for us when we are over fifty. I now know that we really are all one—that we experience life, death, grief, joy, pain, and love. I now have many, many best friends.

YOUR TURN
Discussion Questions:
1. What is your definition of "friend?" Do you have friends who support you and whom you support?
2. Do you choose friends who agree with you all the time, or do you include as friends those who challenge you?
3. Can women and men be friends? Can they be friends in the same way women are friends with women? Why or why not?

Individual Exercise: *Gratitude*
1. Think about the friends you have had throughout your life. Choose the friend who you think had the greatest positive impact on your life.
2. Write a poem expressing gratitude to your friend.
3. Call your friend and read the poem to him or her. If the friend is now deceased, call another friend, explain your purpose—to honor your missing friend—and read the poem.

Group Exercise: *Women Bonding*
1. As a group, watch a movie about female friendships such as "Divine Secrets of the YaYa Sisterhood" or "Waiting to Exhale."
2. What are the messages about friendship, particularly women's friendships, in the movie?
3. How do the themes of the movie relate to your own experiences of women's friendships?

Assignment:
Pretend you are the fourth author of *Saving the Best for Last* and write your story about "Friendship."

Why We Wrote This Book

RENEE

Back in the 60s, I let my hair grow down almost to my butt. I wore long dresses, granny glasses, water buffalo sandals. I marched for peace in Vietnam and sported a black armband to my college graduation. I attended peace rallies, folk concerts and a rock concert where I slept in a tent on a field and got to see Janis Joplin in the flesh. I did *not* practice free love, spend those years in a pot-induced fog or run off to either San Francisco or a commune. My default, deep within the recesses of my being, was to always stay just shy of pushing the limits. I came from a relatively trauma-free childhood and would grow into a relatively trauma-free adulthood.

When the three of us first started having book signings for our first book, *Invisible No More: The Secret Lives of Women Over 50*, I sometimes joked that I was the "boring one." I am neither a survivor of childhood abuse nor of adult breast cancer. The major traumas of my life are ones that many women share: the death of my mother and of a close friend, the dissolution of my marriage. The achievements of my life do not include work for international organizations or creating public policy or being on TV. My most visible position was president of the PTA. Aside from speaking at PTA meetings, my largest audience was three little human beings who seemed to be not listening to anything I said.

I realize now that I did a disservice to myself. I am not the "boring" one. My life is full, rich, challenging. It has simply been played on a stage that is small with a script that has, thank goodness, presented little drama. It is for this very reason that I wrote this book. I am the Everywoman to whom so many others can relate.

My journey has now led me to the inevitable watershed that age bestows: the enormous leap we women make when our bodies move us from childbearing and child raising into a territory that is not only unknown but can be downright scary.

Maybe today you've pulled the visor down at a red light and looked in that little mirror and wondered how much an eye job would cost. Or maybe you told your husband or boyfriend you didn't want to be on top anymore during sex. Or maybe you just heard someone say, "Ma'am?" and you looked around and there wasn't anyone there but you. It's happening to all of us, and it's the stuff of tears-down-your-cheeks-laughter. That's part of this book, of course. But it's not the most important part.

What's important is that you can laugh your guts out at the absurdity of getting older, and, while you are laughing, still know how totally incredible you are. And then, when you're finished laughing, get up, and turn the world on its ass. Or take on a physical challenge you swore you'd never be able to do. Or stand in front of a mirror naked, and know that for some lucky guy, you're a dream come true. Or, at the very least, look at a calendar and circle your birthday and say, "Damn, am I lucky or what?"

JOYCE

All my life I wanted to be older. I wanted to hurry up and be eighteen so I could be truly independent. I thought that as I got older I would be smarter, more self-assured, more daring, more engaging, more in control of my life, more *something*. There was always something more waiting for me beyond whatever my current age happened to be. I thought aging was great!

Turning fifty was remarkable to me. When I turned fifty, I threw a party to beat all birthday parties. It was the first birthday celebration I ever gave myself! At my party, I had a "croning" ceremony, officially conferring on me the right to be a wise, old woman. I thought this was the thing to do, even though I did not feel particularly wise, and I certainly didn't feel old. I still felt like I was in my thirties. I remember silently wondering at the time, "How am I supposed to feel?" After all, I was getting old, wasn't I?

Although aging has not been about numbers for me, getting older has brought wisdom, confidence, self-sufficiency, laudable risks, halting mistakes, peacefulness and laughter. Aging has also created opportunities I never thought possible, and challenges once considered insurmountable.

I embrace the notion that my generation is changing the face of aging. At any age, at any stage in our lives we can create powerful possibilities for ourselves and others. In my experience, it wasn't until I was in my mid-fifties that I began to stop taking my life for granted and began creating the life I truly wanted. My life has surged since turning fifty, and I am grateful for all the women friends I have shared the journey with.

I actually like the word girlfriend rather than woman friend. Girlfriend connotes a much deeper subtext. Girlfriend goes back to my youth, where I met my lifelong friends; it implies intimacy and companionship, a confidant, buddy, playmate and accomplice. Girlfriends are relationships that endure, sustaining us because we love each other and know that no matter how long we may go without talking, we are always connected. Nothing can break the bonds between girlfriends.

Girlfriends are loveable because we recognize our idiosyncrasies, neuroses, and quirks, and accept the entire personality anyway. I do not try to change my girlfriends. My girlfriends represent timeless, ageless connections to my roots, whether the roots are from my youth or the roots of who I am becoming.

For many of us, the way we are now is the way we were as girls with our girlfriends. We share our relationships about men, the dramas we make up in our minds to explain the way men behave, and our amazement that men do not think the way we do. We trouble talk about what is going on in our lives, our goals, our dreams, our families, our confusions, and our concerns. We listen compassionately and provide support and comfort. We laugh uproariously when we are sad and cry when we are happy.

And no matter where we are, or what we are up to, we take the time to check in with each other and share our anxieties, challenges, and secrets we would never reveal to anyone else but our girlfriends. Together we are vulnerable with each other in ways we can never be with men.

These days in our sixties, we've added some new topics related to aging. We commiserate and laugh about our changing bodies and their so-called betrayals; we share our less-than-mature behavior and thoughts, and how we still act (or want to act) on them; and we still talk about sex and/or the lack thereof.

The only thing that has ever held me back is my old belief about aging and how it's "supposed to be." Thank goodness for girlfriends, because in these trusting relationships we get to calm our racing thoughts, explore new ways to look at ourselves and the world, open up our secrets and discover we are not alone, and receive the message that we really are wonderful.

This book sprang from the joy and laughter and tears of my friendships with Jean and Renee and countless others. It is about the joy and laughter and tears of women celebrating and embracing aging.

JEAN

Much of my adult life has been spent with women who are younger than I, partly because I started my professional career in my mid-thirties. One result of this dynamic is that when I headed toward fifty and my physical body began changing, I had no one to talk to about it. I, who used to win the 100-yard dash, was now the slowest runner on my softball team. My hair, which had turned white in my thirties, was no longer prematurely and charmingly so. And then the usual physical changes began: my chin lost its firmness and my eyelids and everything else that could sag began to sag.

By 1999, when I was approaching sixty, my inner and outer selves seemed to belong to two different people. My spirit was complete, confident, and energetic. My physical self was moving in on senior citizen status.

I started reading the literature that existed about women over fifty. First, there was the "geriatric" literature. According to this literature, my future consisted of decay, reduced intellect, and depression. The problem is that all of the research leading to those conclusions was based on studies done in the 1970s of lonely old men who were living in nursing homes. I've been in those homes, and I've seen people staring for hours at blank walls. Talk about depressing! My brain would shrink too with no activity to engage in, and nothing expected of me. But how could that be the model for my future?

There were some other voices. Groups like the Gray Panthers were writing about the rights of seniors. They were using the civil rights confrontation model to combat discrimination. Their view of life was an "us against them" view: a paradigm that served well in the struggle for racial justice; but, in my mind, it didn't work as a useful way for women over fifty to view life.

There were some feminist writers on the verge of discovering that being over fifty could mean a whole new way of being. In the 1960s, while on book tours for *The Feminine Mystique*, Betty Friedan held meetings with women around the country. She asked questions about menopause and wanted to know just how awful it was. She heard that for some women, menopause happened, but without all of the serious physical manifestations that were then thought to exist for all women. These were all women who had stepped out of, or expanded on, the traditional wife/mother roles. Friedan's thought was that maybe it was because these women were "living large" that they were not suffering the expected physical effects of menopause.

With the exception of those skeletal but intriguing thoughts from Friedan, as I too never "experienced" menopause, I found little in the literature that was reflecting my experience. I was bothered by my physical changes, but very excited about my future. So, I started talking with women. I talked with women in high political positions in government and women who worked in the cafeteria. I talked with single women, married women, straight women, and lesbian women. I talked with mothers about their daughters' lives and with daughters about their mothers' lives. I talked with lawyers, songwriters, authors, artists, and dancers. I talked with women who started organizations that were having an impact on the world and with women who had never worked outside of the home.

What I heard from these women indicated to me that a shift is occurring at this very moment in history. The shift is in how women over fifty view themselves. Society was saying what they should be feeling was the move to retirement: to slowing down, releasing, resting. That the business of motherhood was done and the business of career was done. This message is reflected everywhere from the media to birthday cards: you are on the downward slope or over the hill. Contrary to this notion, the women I talked with were feeling the desire to move, grow, shine, write the book, paint the picture, change the world, have the love affair, learn to dance, start the foundation, go to Bali, cut the hair short, become a healer, travel the world. All were ready to radically shift direction.

I found an experience of dissonance in these women between a constantly enriching inner self and an aging physical body. I asked them about the "falling apart" side of being over fifty. Those women who had strong notions about what they wanted to do for the rest of their lives, who had a strong sense of themselves as being filled with potential for an exciting future, were less anxious about the changes. It wasn't that they weren't experiencing the changes. In fact, they noticed them and didn't like them; but, on the whole, they had bigger things to talk about.

The more I listened, the more fascinated I became. Each of the women welcomed my introducing the topic with excitement and positive energy. Not one woman said, "I want to retire. I want only to go home and knit booties for my grandchildren. I want only to sit in my garden." Many women did not know what it was they wanted, but they were clear that they were in a search and that their direction was growth and change, not retirement.

I knew then that I was lucky enough to be living in a time in which profound social change was occurring. I am a member of a population group that is the untapped resource for change in this society. I am part of a group of women who have lived past the expectations of society regarding marriage and child rearing. We have outlived the old concepts of the purpose of women. We are past the politics of it now. We have lived long enough to go beyond the biological imperative.

We are on the edge of a largely unnoticed revolution. Everyone knows the concept of "baby-boomer," but no one really has gotten what that means for women. This is a revolution without blood, without anger, without hostility. This is a societal, psychological, and spiritual revolution. And because we are women, our energy will take us in the direction of peace, nurture, and love. This is damned exciting.

Within the first year after my awakening in 1999, I retired early from my senior executive job and became a model and actor. I landed a contract that has me traveling to Prague on business. I present workshops called "Women of a Certain Age" in which women near or over age fifty get to declare what they want to do with the rest of their lives. This year I was a finalist to be on the "Survivor" television show. I would have been the oldest woman ever on the show.

I want conversations about us "women of a certain age" on everyone's lips. I want to redefine life. I want to redefine beauty. I want to redefine sex. I want to redefine love. Joyce, Renee, and I meet periodically for breakfast. Our discussions are marked by, and saturated with, laughter. It's the laughter of love, shared experience, and excitement about our lives. I want such conversations to go on all over the country as we laugh at ourselves, and at life, as we begin to appreciate and celebrate who we are at this stage in our lives.

YOUR TURN

Discussion Questions:

1. What will your legacy be, and why does it matter?
2. What is your role in the world?
3. What do you care about?

Individual Exercise: *Commit to Yourself*

This exercise has several purposes:

- to have your intentions be real and important to you
- to have you commit to your intentions
- to have something to reference on those days when you aren't sure what your life is about
- to experience the joy of completion when you accomplish your goal.

1. Write a Letter of Commitment (LOC). An LOC represents your commitments to yourself over the next year. The LOC should cover what you consider to be the major areas of your life: *e.g.*, career, relationships, finances. In each area, state your goal for the year.
2. Put the date by which each goal will be accomplished. If there are major steps to the goal, put in dates for them also. Make all goals measurable: "how many by when."
3. If possible, do this exercise with a friend. Bi-weekly or monthly, report to each other on your progress toward your goals.

Group Exercise: *In Memory of You*

This exercise will focus you on whether you are on track with your life's vision. It also will serve to support you to create everything you want in your life.

1. Each person in the group will write her obituary. Do not identify yourself on the document.
2. The obituary should be no longer than one page but should include everything about your life for which you want to be remembered. Allow no more than ten minutes for this exercise.
3. When everyone has completed this exercise, fold the papers in quarters and put them in a container.
4. Each person will pull one paper from the container. One at a time, read the obituaries out loud. After each one, the group

will attempt to determine whose obituary has been read.

5. Discuss the experience of writing your own obituary and of hearing it read. Did it surprise you how many or how few people recognized your obituary?

Assignment:

Pretend you are the fourth author of *Saving the Best for Last* and write your story about "Why I Wrote This Book."

Renee Fisher has been writing fiction and poetry since childhood. In 2001 her novel, King of the Gypsies, was published through iUniverse. She has had several short stories published in literary magazines, including Kingfisher and Metropolitain. She is an Honorable Mention in the Lorian Hemingway Short Story Competition. She is currently working on her second novel.

Formerly an artist and special education teacher, she has been a Realtor in the Washington, D.C. area since 1979. She is currently a Top Producer of the Northern Virginia Association of Realtors. In addition, in 2000 she started the first non-denominational speed dating company, Brief Encounters USA, and presently is involved in the startup of a brand new company "Diva Diversions."

Joyce Kramer taught English in inner city Baltimore for twenty-five years. After retiring, she became Director of Volunteer Services and later Director of Development and Public Relations of the first major community-based HIV/AIDS organization in Maryland. She followed her work in Baltimore with a position as Development and Public Relations Director at the National Association of People with AIDS in Washington, D.C.

In her mid-fifties, Joyce began her third career incarnation when she became a self-employed consultant on global HIV/AIDS and health broadcasting in Washington, DC. She traveled to East Africa to research and write case studies on anti-vaccination rumors in three countries.

Jean Peelen is a women's advocate, civil rights attorney, policy writer, model, actress, radio show host, and "Women of a Certain Age" workshop leader. She is the author of Federal policy documents on subjects including the rights of women and girls in sports, the desegregation of public schools, and sexual harassment in schools and colleges. Jean published management articles in The Public Manager, such as "How to Fire a Federal Employee and Stay Sane."

Jean left a position as Chief of Staff of a Federal agency to become an advocate of the power and possibility of women over fifty. At age fifty-nine, she became a successful model and commercial actor in New York, Philadelphia, and Washington, D.C. Jean also is a National Spokesperson for The Sister Study, funded by the National Institutes of Health, to study sisters of women who have had breast cancer. In this position, she is speaking to "women of a certain age" across the country.

Breinigsville, PA USA
25 February 2010
233194BV00004B/2/P